Praise for *Involution*

"A vital document of contemporary labor that finds, in eight Chinese lives, a story unfolding wherever a degree no longer buys the future it promised."

Eric Blanc, author of *We Are the Union*

"When we read about China's youth unemployment crisis or the 'lying flat' meme, we rarely encounter the lives behind the headlines. By gathering the stories of young workers—from a teacher in Hunan to a debt collector in Jilin—*Involution* offers us an essential and deeply human glimpse into their experiences. Thanks to Friedman's attentive translation, readers beyond China can come to understand the struggles that so many young Chinese face in their pursuit of dignified work and a decent life."

Yi-Ling Liu, author of *The Wall Dancers*

"*Involution* offers simple yet profound narratives of Chinese youth's work and life in the current era, reflecting both the material and spiritual crises of Gen Z in China and beyond. While not producing the stories as a political text, by highlighting these stories the book calls for co-experience, co-identification, and co-research with the working class, blurring the boundaries between blue-collar and white-collar and transgressing the defining limits of job and joblessness to nurture solidarity."

Pun Ngai, author of *Made in China*

HUNDRED FLOWERS

In 1956, seven years after his victory in China's Communist Revolution, Mao Zedong extended an invitation to the country's intelligentsia: "Let a hundred flowers bloom, let a hundred different schools of thought contend." As criticism of the Chinese Communist Party swelled, the Hundred Flowers project morphed into something cynical, known as the Anti-Rightist Campaign. As a result, many who had, in good faith, produced texts and essays critical of the party faced repression; many careers were destroyed.

Verso's Hundred Flowers series aims to fulfill Mao's promise in earnest by publishing writing on China from the mainland, the diaspora, and elsewhere. Once a key American ally, China has emerged over the course of this century as the only serious challenger to US global economic hegemony. Yet China remains largely opaque to the West, which is too often ignorant of both the country's history and its contemporary internal dynamics. Books, newspaper articles, and magazine essays abound but at best present simplistic views of China; at worst, these accounts are misleading or scaremongering. Hundred Flowers offers a more nuanced perspective to facilitate serious debate in analyzing China's past, present, and future.

Other titles in this series available from Verso Books:

The Unmaking of the Chinese Working Class by Teemu Ruskola
The Women by Yan Lianke

Involution

A Worker Inquiry Amid China's Youth Unemployment Wave

Gonglao Collective

Translation by Eli Friedman

VERSO

London • New York

This English-language edition first published by Verso 2026
First published in China as 青年失业潮下：劳动调查 (Qingnian shiye chao xia: laodong diaochao [Under the Youth Unemployment Wave: Labor Investigation])

The manufacturer's authorized representative in the EU for product safety (GPSR) is LOGOS EUROPE, 9 rue Nicolas Poussin, 17000, La Rochelle, France
contact@logoseurope.eu

1 3 5 7 9 10 8 6 4 2

Verso
UK: 6 Meard Street, London W1F 0EG
US: 207 East 32nd Street, New York, NY 10016
versobooks.com

Verso is the imprint of New Left Books

ISBN-13: 978-1-83674-295-1
ISBN-13: 978-1-83674-297-5 (US EBK)
ISBN-13: 978-1-83674-296-8 (UK EBK)

British Library Cataloguing in Publication Data
A catalogue record for this book is available from the British Library

Library of Congress Cataloging-in-Publication Data

Names: Friedman, Eli translator
Title: Involution : a worker inquiry amid China's youth unemployment wave / Gonglao Collective ; translation by Eli Friedman.
Other titles: 880-01 Qing nian shi ye chao xia. English | 880-64 Gong lao xiao bao
Description: English-language edition. | London ; New York : Verso, 2026. | Series: Hundred flowers | Translation of: 青年失业潮下：劳动调查.
Identifiers: LCCN 2026008364 (print) | LCCN 2026008365 (ebook) | ISBN 9781836742951 paperback | ISBN 9781836742975 US ebk | ISBN 9781836742968 UK ebk
Subjects: LCSH: Young adults—Employment—China | Unemployment—China
Classification: LCC HD6276.C62 G66 2026 (print) | LCC HD6276.C62 (ebook)
LC record available at https://lccn.loc.gov/2026008364
LC ebook record available at https://lccn.loc.gov/2026008365

Typeset in Fournier by Hewer Text UK Ltd, Edinburgh
Printed and bound by CPI Group (UK) Ltd, Croydon, CR0 4YY

Contents

Preface to the English-Language Edition

In 2012, a former Apple executive breathlessly recounted to the *New York Times* their sense of wonder at doing business in China. The article detailed how Apple had decided on a last-minute screen redesign for a new iPhone, putting the production schedule at risk of delay. When the new screens arrived at the Chinese assembly plant around midnight, the factory immediately pulled 8,000 on-site workers from slumber and set them in motion. "The speed and flexibility is breathtaking," marveled the executive.*

Capitalists foreign and domestic have swooned over "China speed"—the officially sanctioned discourse that valorizes the country's superior work ethic and pro-business institutional environment. There is no doubt that the twenty-first-century PRC has innovated new regimes of labor deployment and exploitation that have accelerated the circulation of capital and commodities. Factory and construction workers are housed on-site to eliminate commuting time; compulsory overtime has been normalized for blue- and white-collar workers alike; the potential

---

* Charles Duhigg and Keith Bradsher, "How the US Lost Out on iPhone Work," *New York Times*, January 21, 2012.

friction of trade unions has been eliminated; and an internal migration regime has resulted in 300 million people working away from home, relatively unencumbered by familial and social obligations. This socio-political environment has allowed corporations to produce more things in less time, while continually increasing the rate of exploitation and eroding workers' free time.

This acceleration and competition has seeped out of the workplace and into the realm of social reproduction. Parents begin to pressure their children to improve their skillset as early as primary school by enrolling them in evening, weekend, and summer cram schools. The cutthroat competition they will one day face in the labor market is anticipated by even more ruthless competition in their high school and university entrance exams. China's two-decade real estate bubble has made it increasingly difficult for young people to purchase homes. Marriage itself has been reconfigured by these processes of marketization, as a wide swath of society now sees home and car ownership as prerequisites to matrimony. Whether in the workplace, school, or the home, Chinese youth have been inundated with competitive pressures from all directions.

"Involution" (*neijuan* 内卷) is the term young people in China have adopted to refer to this multidimensional socio-economic strain. As conceptualized by anthropologist Clifford Geertz, involution is a dynamic of intensification and growing complexity without progress. Plucking it from its original academic setting, Chinese youth have breathed new life and meaning into the term. For this new generation, involution describes a sense of futility in the face of ratcheting demands for self-improvement, increases in productivity, and wealth accumulation; it evokes a feeling of being trapped in a centripetal doom spiral. As in Geertz's original conceptualization, this intensification of competition does not result in forward movement for Chinese youth, at either the individual or societal level. In other words, despite China's growing wealth, young people increasingly feel that their efforts have been detached from outcomes.

This new common sense presents a stark departure from the cultural outlook of the previous generation. China's world-altering capitalist boom created immense opportunities over the past forty years, and even as the country's levels of inequality increased, most people saw improvements in their material well-being. This was particularly the case for university graduates, the subject of this book. Following the bloody repression of the pro-democracy movement in 1989, the state struck an implicit bargain with China's youth: Those who were willing to abandon political idealism and able to get into university could expect economic prosperity. Historically unprecedented growth, especially after 1992, allowed the state to deliver on this promise, and an entire generation of university grads expressed great optimism about their own future and that of the nation. As late as the mid-2010s the common sense on university campuses and in society more broadly was one of teleological *progress*—a belief rooted in the lived experience of much of the population.

It was, nonetheless, a belief dependent on a particular and ephemeral political economy. In addition to infrastructural development and supply chain magic, "China speed" could just as easily refer to the country's rapid development. In a process that played out over centuries in western Europe, China has gone from a poor agrarian society to a global superpower, and it's now leading technological innovation in a variety of fields. This accelerated historical timeline means that each of the past three generations has confronted a radically different world. Today's elders grew up amid deprivation and perhaps the twentieth century's worst famine, only to see new opportunities emerge in the private labor-intensive factories that began popping up in the 1980s. Middle-aged people who reached adulthood in the prosperous 1990s and 2000s enjoyed educational and employment opportunities that their parents could not have dreamed of. For many in this generation, studying hard was a plausible pathway to a white-collar job, a modern apartment that doubled as a rapidly appreciating asset, and various other material and cultural trappings of middle-class life. Especially for those fortunate enough to get a university education, there was ample evidence to support an ideology of linear progress.

The neck-snapping shift from the optimism of the 2000s and 2010s to today's pessimism has been catalyzed by two key dynamics: a massive increase in access to higher education and a decline in economic prospects. In the 1980s and '90s, tertiary education was reserved for a small segment of the population. China was following the historically recognizable pattern of agrarian transformation and industrialization, and state leadership had identified abundant and cheap labor as their comparative advantage in development. While China was still industrializing, the state already had its eyes on the next phase of growth, one they presumed to be more dependent on efficiency gains and innovation. This led to an admirable drive to dramatically expand access to higher education. In 2000, China's gross enrollment rate for tertiary education was under 8 percent.* But after two decades of heavy state investment, by 2020 it had climbed to over 54 percent, with nearly 42 million students enrolled in higher education.† The families of these growing millions expected that a university degree would open pathways of prosperity.

But the structure of China's economy has been shifting under the feet of these graduates, and the rapid growth in university enrollment has outpaced growth of good jobs. Economic difficulty and rising joblessness during the pandemic were assumed to be temporary hardships. But when massive protests by workers and students pushed the government to end chaotically implemented and socially regressive lockdowns in late 2022, the economy did not roar back to life. In fact, youth unemployment continued to rise, climbing to 21.3 percent in June 2023. Faced with the breakdown of their generation-long agreement with the middle class to provide economic returns in exchange for political acquiescence, the government panicked; in August 2023 they announced a pause in reporting youth unemployment data. The stated reason was that they needed to

* "China, School Enrollment, Tertiary (% Gross)," IndexMundi.com, accessed June 22, 2025.

† "Major educational achievements in China in 2020," *Ministry of Education*, February 28, 2021.

refine their methodology, but everyone understood it as an attempt to withhold bad news. In January 2024 the new methodology produced a more favorable, but still high, youth unemployment rate of 14.9 percent. Regardless, the state's actions only generated greater resentment among unemployed youth, who had a growing sense that state was more interested in hiding the problem than addressing its causes.

At the same time, the jobs that were available had become increasingly demanding while the cost of living had skyrocketed. There is no question that China's corporate champions—including companies like BYD, Huawei, Alibaba, and Tencent—were developing innovative commodities and winning greater market share, domestically and globally. But they and other private firms weren't creating enough middle-class jobs, and the jobs they did create were far from ideal. Without unions or adequate legal protection, many workers are now subjected to the notorious 996 work schedule (9 a.m. to 9 p.m., six days a week) with no capacity to resist recurrent waves of layoffs. While wages have grown significantly over the past generation, the cost of living in large cities has ballooned as well. For young people without family wealth, it has been nearly impossible to get into the housing market in places like Beijing or Shenzhen. Pensions and public eldercare are woefully inadequate, which means that elders are often highly dependent on the support of their children—a huge proportion of whom have no siblings. Childcare is a private affair, and middle-class parents see costly tutoring for their kids as an obligatory expense. In short, those lucky enough to land good jobs in the service sector have continued to face intense work demands *and* spiraling costs for largely privatized social reproduction. With Xi Jinping categorically opposed to the creation of a robust welfare state, the latter issue is unlikely to subside.

Undergirding this dynamic is a secular slowdown in economic growth. Although China fared well in the aftermath of the 2008 economic crisis via massive investment in infrastructure and real estate, its growth rate has steadily declined from the double-digit figures of the boom years. More recently, the government has aimed for "around 5 percent" growth, a number they inevitably meet one way or another. The sectors driving the economy—notably tech, renewables, and EVs—have not created a broad base of prosperity. Manufacturing has become increasingly automated, and competition is savage: In 2024, eighty-six brands produced EVs in China, with only a small minority turning a profit.* This market environment has resulted in price wars, downward pressure on wages, increased demands on output, and regular layoffs. Judging by market share, China's companies were experiencing incredible success by the early 2020s. But this emergent commercial empire has not been enough to sustain high growth or to create a hefty demographic of high consumers. As economists of all ideological perspectives have noted since the early 2000s, without increased domestic consumption and reduced reliance on exports and investment, China's

* Brian Thevenot and Victoria Waldersee, "China's Cutthroat EV Revolution Leaves Little Room for Profit," Reuters.com, accessed June 29, 2025.

economy will continue to be sapped of vitality. But the lack of broadly distributed wealth is a political problem that the state will not solve on its own.

The Gonglao Collective is a product of this historical moment. Made up of activists within China and in the diaspora, this group formed in 2022 with the simple aim of collecting and distributing information about China's workers. Since then, they have expanded their activities to include reports on workers' online discussions as well as the kind of interview research that forms the basis of this book. The name Gonglao (工劳) can be read as a contraction formed by the first characters of worker (*gongren* 工人) and labor (*laogong* 劳工). As they note in their introduction, *gong* comes first to highlight that it is *workers* who do the labor to create society. In a media and political environment that is generally hostile to labor, simply presenting workers' experiences, in their own voices, is a radical act. Their website has already become an invaluable resource on labor conditions and worker resistance in China at a moment when channels of information have been badly diminished due to repression and censorship. Gonglao aims for this information to serve as a foundation for worker solidarity across divides of profession, gender, and ethnicity.

Published in late 2024, *Involution* was the group's first print publication and an important milestone in establishing their leadership in activist research. Foreign readers might see the politics expressed in the book as relatively tame—there are only mild critiques of government policy, and the politics espoused by most interviewees are hardly radical—but no official publishers in China would want to risk putting it out. The independently published book is not for sale in bookstores within China and can only be purchased in a handful of locations internationally.

Gonglao's decision to focus their first book on unemployment and university graduates represents a major intellectual shift in China's labor activism and research. As in other countries, workers in manufacturing have had a privileged place in the imaginary of labor activists in China. From the 2000s on, scholars and activists were increasingly focused on rural-to-urban migrant workers in private enterprises rather than the traditional Maoist working class in state-owned enterprises. Despite the peak of manufacturing employment in the mid-2000s, many believed that factory workers were the most likely group to lead whatever labor movement would emerge in China's capitalist transition. By the 2010s and even more so in the early 2020s, more researchers and activists were attending to workers in the sectors of service, transportation, sanitation, and especially platform-based deliveries. But in all cases, there has been an assumption that "workers" referred to blue-collar workers, typically people with only a primary or secondary school education.

With this book, Gonglao has made an implicit argument that university graduates ought to be considered part of the working class, and therefore that they should be on the intellectual and practical agenda for labor activists. The collective's position is never articulated as such (aside from a passing comment about the "blue collarization of white-collar work" in the editorial notes), indicating their hesitancy about how precisely to think about the class position or political role of China's highly educated workers. This indeterminacy is reflected in some of the worker narratives, too, which evince the interviewees' confusion about their own class positions. This is particularly clear in Chapter 1 where we learn about the experiences of an intern at a debt collection company. One of the few interviewees who is an avowed leftist, they talk about identifying as a "worker" and a "proletarian"—understandable given the brutal speedup and exploitation they encountered while working for the company. Curiously, however, the chapter concludes with the interviewee suggesting that to realize their radical political ideals, they "want to understand workers' lives," and that the way to accomplish that will be to get a job in a factory. It is as if their own experiences as a worker (in an office) did not register as such. While consciously, and understandably, avoiding firm analytical conclusions, Gonglao has made an invaluable contribution by raising the question of white-collar workers' position in class politics. The current transformation of China's economy and class structure will ensure that this issue will only become more important in the years to come.

Labor activist and scholar Weixiang Chen has expressed guarded optimism about the potential for coalitional labor politics embedded in China's 2022 anti-lockdown protests. Beginning in the spring of that year, blue-collar migrant workers revolted against the "closed loop" management systems where they were locked inside factories and forced to work to ensure that capital could circulate amid the pandemic. In the fall, even more spectacular protests occurred in migrant communities in Guangzhou and the "iPhone City" in Zhengzhou, where thousands of workers battled police and pandemic enforcement officers to demand food, medicine, and freedom. Shortly thereafter, a wave of protests by students and professionals engulfed China's campuses and largest cities, with young people demanding an end to the lockdowns while many held blank pieces of paper to dramatize their opposition to censorship. Chen argues that although these movements took place in parallel, they reflect an important shift in China's class structure. Those young "white paper" protestors were willing to risk repression precisely because they no longer felt that a university degree and a white-collar job would ensure them the future they desired. Their increasing precarity was bringing them closer structurally, if not yet socially, to the underclass of migrant proletarians.

Although the social divide between white- and blue-collar workers remains formidable, there are some emergent cultural similarities between them. Rejection of involution, the valorization of withdrawal from the labor market, and disillusion with societal norms have also surfaced among China's marginalized rural-to-urban migrants. This phenomenon first broke into the national consciousness several years ago via media reports on the "Sanhe Gods" (三和大神).*
The "Gods" are a community of migrants in Shenzhen who

---

* I am indebted to Zhuang Han for his insightful analyses of the Sanhe Gods.

take on temporary day labor and work as little as possible, embracing the maxim "work one day, hang out for three." These workers have determined that, given the jobs available, they will never be able to save enough to realize the social expectations of marriage and homeownership. Rather than killing themselves via involutionary competition, they work as little as possible, reduce their expenditures to an absolute minimum, and forsake the pursuit of mainstream respectability. While only a small number of people identify as Sanhe Gods, this subaltern antiwork ethos has found broad resonance for millions of young people with diverse class positions.

Involution, based on research less than a year after the 2022 protests, does not provide evidence of a budding alliance between downwardly mobile university grads and blue-collar migrant workers. But as with the Sanhe Gods, it does reveal the deeply unsettled psychic terrain that China's educated youth inhabit, and their loss of faith in the prevailing authoritarian capitalist order to deliver a decent life. One of the most notable themes in the book is the deep sense of pessimism and emotional strain these young people are managing. Many recent college grads have moved back in with their families, and while they might not have to wonder where their next meal will come from, they are adrift. Throughout this book, people refer to themselves as feeling *mimang* (迷茫), a term that literally means "confused," while indicating a sense of unbounded haziness. For nearly two generations, China has been laser-focused on *development*: Both at the national and individual level, the mission was to secure the material basis of modern living, providing people with a crisply defined aim to strive for. But the youth whose families have realized this goal are now left with the challenge of maintaining their class position and maybe even seeking personal fulfillment. Through some combination of privilege and grit the people in this book have succeeded academically, only to feel unmoored in life. This pervasive angst is a pattern familiar to people in other rich countries in the West and East Asia: Capitalism can deliver material bounty to some, but the end of development doesn't promise a meaningful existence.

Perhaps Chinese youth culture's most successful export has been the idea, or even the ideal, of "lying flat" (*tangping* 躺平), a theme repeatedly discussed in this book. Along with *mimang*, lying flat should be read as a cultural response to spiraling competition (i.e., involution) in all spheres of society. As white-collar work has become increasingly precarious and unable to provide personal fulfillment or a socially valorized lifestyle, people are looking for an exit. Lying flat represents a call to reject the norms of competition, hard work, property ownership, and the heteronormative family for a life of minimal effort and maximum leisure (albeit in a materially constrained manner). This antiwork discourse has spooked capitalists and political elites, with everyone from Jack Ma to Xi Jinping reminding young people that hard work is the path to success. Moral panic notwithstanding, China remains a capitalist society in which work is the only way that people can secure their means of survival. In other words, the lying flat discourse is an important *cultural* development in that it signals growing disillusionment with exploitative labor practices and social competition more broadly. But it is also inherently an individualized reaction to a social problem. *Social* withdrawal from capitalist exploitation remains an enormous political task, and lying flat will remain in the realm of utopian longing or marginal lifestyle politics for the foreseeable future.

Chinese youth have developed a variety of other individualized responses to involution. Employment in the civil service or in state-owned companies is perhaps the most obvious shelter from the market tempest. But as the narratives in this book attest, competition for these jobs is unimaginably stiff, while a growing share of employment in both government and state-owned enterprises (SOEs) has become more precarious via outsourcing and flexibilization. "Runology" (*runxue* 润学), i.e., the science of running away to another country, is another trend that has been widely discussed online. Emigration has indeed ticked up in recent years and has provided a degree of safety for many people fleeing political persecution. Many émigrés are also rich people seeking to stash their wealth in Dubai real estate or family offices in Singapore; those hoping for a more humane labor market overseas are likely to be disappointed. Political refugees are also encountering a more hostile global landscape, particularly for those in the United States who fear deportation and likely jail time back in China.

The youth interviewed in this book are, to one degree or another, dissatisfied and anxious about work and their future. They are also grappling with how to respond and are generally clear-eyed about the limitations of lying flat.

Several people express demands for government and educational institutions to do more to alleviate their hardship. But the kinds of fixes they can envision remain quite limited. The procurement officer in Chapter 7 is the most explicit in calling for greater worker resistance to exploitation. Nonetheless, when we look carefully at her political vision, it is confined to filing legal grievances against unscrupulous employers. And her greatest hope for the future is to get a job at a foreign-owned company, which she believes will be better than Chinese companies. The leftist in Chapter 1 ends by saying they want to get a job in a factory, but they have no concrete plans for worker organizing. Since the brutal and encompassing repression against student labor activists in 2018–19, the field of political imagination and practice has been severely constrained.

Despite these unique political conditions, the economic stagnation and social dissolution experienced by youth in China are rooted in the same process of global capitalist degeneration that has produced homologous effects in the rich countries of Euro-America and East Asia. While China, somewhat improbably, has a higher youth unemployment rate, the phenomena of precarious employment, out-of-control housing costs, and refusal of marriage and child-rearing are equally familiar to university graduates in Taiwan and South Korea, Spain and the UK, the United States and Canada. And these countries have similarly seen a rise in youth depression and anxiety about the future. While the intensity of socio-economic pressure is uneven, and each place has its own distinct cultural expressions, it is apparent that involution names a problem as global as capital. This means that there is a material, if not yet ideological, basis for developing political solidarities across the imperial divide.

In Chapter 5, a teacher from Hunan says that involution is "based on the idea that we should see other people as enemies." When we listen closely to the workers in this book, as Gonglao has implored us to do, we can detect a common rejection of this generalized enmity. Our aim, as always, is to cohere individual anguish into collective politics so that we may build a world predicated on cooperation.

Eli Friedman

Editors' Note

Brecht cut to the heart of the matter when he asked, "Who built Thebes with its seven gates? / Books say it was kings. / Did kings hew and haul the rock?"* The answer is obvious. Although traditional Chinese morality seems to passionately promote humility and deflect credit, there are always some information gaps that make people suddenly feel confused. Who built the cities? Who makes modern life function? Did we grow the vegetables on the shelves of the supermarket ourselves?

However, even as consumer subjects we become conscious that there is nothing inevitable about the convenience of daily modern life. We still don't know how to recognize and understand the workers who make this type of life possible. With consumption and production so distant, even if we "see," the object of our gaze remains invisible.

When we try to see the people who have been obscured from our daily life, we might look at some questionable numbers released by the statistics bureau; or occasionally a

* Bertolt Brecht, "A Worker Reads and Asks," trans. Oliver Reynolds, Poem of the Week, TLS.com, accessed May 4, 2025.

personal literary narrative when some lucky child of the working class gains some ephemeral exposure; or on Douyin or Kuaishou we might glimpse the exoticized "lower strata" subjected to a voyeuristic gaze consumed with the grotesque spectacle;* or the middle class may reflect on its own privileges to signal its sympathy with the other; This, of course, is insufficient.

Because these encounters are all accidental and passive.

Why then, did we create Gonglao? Why are we called Gonglao? It isn't because our editorial department is full of people who don't understand grammar, but rather that we want to bring a bit more respect and understanding to the character *gong*, the worker.† Who is doing the labor? It is the *worker*. All Gonglao wants to do is to see the worker.

This is our reason for conducting this survey and interview project: Allowing Foxconn workers to discuss their own dissatisfactions, allowing taxi, truck, and on-demand drivers to tell of their difficulties, allowing workers to tell us in their own words about the evil of labor brokers, why they hate male bosses, how hard it is to find work, how hard life can be, and what should be done about it.

Perhaps there isn't any brilliant Marxist theorization here, and there aren't any complex mathematical models to quantify the social situation of workers. Lots of people

---

* Douyin is the PRC's version of TikTok; Kuaishou is also a short video-based social media app.

† Gonglao (工劳) playfully reverses the order of the two characters that make up the word "labor" (*laogong*劳工), in a way that, as they indicate, might make the word look like a typo.

are already working on such things, and we are just writing a relatively minor report. It is our hope that this comparatively brief report will play a part in bringing some attention to the perspective of people too often overlooked.

1

Diary of an Intern at a Debt Collection Agency: Overwork, Stress, and Seven Hundred Phone Calls

I'm from Jilin, now in my junior year at university. Officially my school is a third-tier university, but I feel like it's basically a vocational college. The school arranges internships and we get to pick from a few companies. Now I'm interning at a debt collection agency.

Student Sun from Jilin, 2024 graduate

The Job Is Bullshit, and Employees Curse the Company Every Day

All I do every day is call people to collect debts. I take the bus to work a little after eight and don't get off work till seven or eight at night, then I head back to the dorm to sleep. Every day is the same cycle. I get five or six days off per month and a base wage of 2,000 yuan, with performance pay calculated separately.

My internship isn't really related to my major, which is finance. I'm over here doing debt-collection calls, so I guess it's a little related [laughs]. My school hired some labor intermediaries, and they got in touch with this company. There are thirty or forty of us in this group and we all come from the same college. The company has been working with the school for five or six years and they get about this many interns every year.

This is such a bullshit internship. We're under crazy pressure every day. We have to work ten or more hours. Management sets a quota, and we complete the tasks. The quotas can change anytime. We have to make seven hundred phone calls per day and spend five and a half hours on calls or waiting while the phone is ringing, otherwise they will deduct 50 yuan.* Aside from this there are also a lot of deductions for quality control based on the content of the calls. They can deduct 30 to 200 yuan; the biggest fines are up to 1,000.

Workers' positions are divided between regular and small accounts. The difference between the two is mostly their targets and salary. The regular workers have higher demands, with higher requirements for performance pay, but their salaries are also relatively high. Small accounts workers don't have any pressure from performance pay and they aren't managed too harshly. After they finish their calls they can leave work. But when it comes to fines, everyone is treated equally. The majority are regular employees, and they have a lot of pressure. The workplace is super oppressive, nobody gets time to rest—once you're there,

* Seven hundred calls in a 10.5-hour day seems impossible if employees are expected to converse with the debtors. Nonetheless, that is what Sun has said here.

you're making phone calls. After a half-hour break in the middle of the day, you have to keep at it so you can finish with work sooner rather than later. A lot of the regular employees want to switch to small accounts positions because they can't take the pressure. My performance demands weren't that bad in August. When I started out, I wasn't doing small accounts. But later I couldn't keep up with the work, and for the final ten days of the month I switched to small accounts. I'm also doing small accounts this month—small accounts are cases with debts of less than 1,000 yuan. Most interns want to do small accounts, but the normal employees they recruit don't want the small ones, they're here to make money. Us interns aren't as constrained by financial need.

Among my classmates in this program, there is a huge range in terms of their performance. Some students' output is good, and they get high performance pay (one even earned 10,000 yuan), and some is much lower, just over 1,000 yuan, for example. Then there are those like me who don't want to earn too much money and therefore take the small accounts so that things are a little more relaxed—especially since it was recently Mid-Autumn Festival and National Day and we didn't get any vacation.*

My classmates all hate this job. Every day we're just sitting there cursing the company. But we're required to intern for six months to get our diploma, so we just have to grin and bear it. I heard that in the previous class there was a student who led a revolt. Apparently, they were a strong

* These are both major national holidays in China.

organizer and people were so dissatisfied that a big group of them quit their internships. It seems like the school didn't punish them afterward. The school hasn't revealed any info about this. I've also thought about trying to contact a labor inspector, but I'm just not very sure how to protect my rights. I recently heard that the company pays the school 1,000 yuan for every student that stays there for three months, but I'm not sure if that's true.

Before starting at the debt collection agency, I also interviewed for other internships including one at China Merchants Bank in Shanghai. It was also a debt collection job, but I wasn't selected. I also tried for a hotel. That would have been even more exhausting as you have to walk 30,000 steps each day.

The Company Has Redefined "Overtime"

The pressure we feel is mostly mental. If your performance isn't good, the company will find all kinds of ways to fuck with you. Yesterday when a client came, all our phones were confiscated and locked up. They didn't allow anything on the table except for cups and napkins. If they saw anything you'd be fined right away. Usually, we're allowed to chat at work, but yesterday our output wasn't good, and our manager cussed us out. They were like, "How dare you smile?" The company has been losing money recently and there have been a lot of issues with quality control. There are three teams altogether, and there have been problems in two of them. Yesterday after 6 p.m. our manager said we're going to have to have meetings all next week.

The company has also redefined overtime. On normal workdays they don't count longer hours as overtime; the only thing that they call "overtime" is when you work on a holiday or weekend—but you still don't get *paid* overtime. Company rules are that you get five or six days off per month. When you take a day off, they give your files to someone else. This becomes a kind of forced overtime since that person then has to put in more hours to complete their performance targets.

If you regularly hit your targets, the company's three most productive employees can get a salary of more than 10,000 yuan per month. The average salary is 5,000 to 6,000 yuan. Those who have lower productivity just get 1,000 yuan.* I've been here for two months and have earned just over 2,000.

I'd estimate that there is about a four-to-six ratio of interns to regular employees. The company has partnerships with more than one school. Just a few days ago I had to move into a new dorm room to make room for a new intern. I told my manager that since I was moving dorms, I wanted fewer cases so I could get off work earlier. But my manager completely ignored me. They said that I should just work faster and it would be fine, I could still get off work by seven. Some new interns will volunteer for overtime to earn a bit more, but now hardly anyone does. I heard that our school's party secretary was going to come to the company to visit us, but it turned out that nobody

* This is far below the minimum wage in every city in China, including in relatively impoverished western regions.

came.* A couple of days ago the school asked us to pay tuition and housing fees. But we're living at the company, so I don't understand why we need to pay the school for housing. What help can the school give us?

The Future Is Uncertain

To be honest, I don't know what I'm going to do in the future. When I was choosing a major I just wanted something that had lower tuition, so I picked finance. I didn't even think about what kinds of courses they'd offer. I had no idea what I wanted to do or what I was interested in. The stuff I learned has been totally irrelevant; it's all just this boring Western economics.

I'm planning to move back home after I finish so I can be close to my family and save on rent. My parents are divorced. My dad lives in the county town and my mom is in the village. During vacations I'm running back and forth between the two places. The village and the city are like two different worlds: The city is more economically developed and the village is so impoverished. The only people left are older farmers and workers; the young people have all left for the city. The only people farming are seniors.

Whatever I do in the future is fine. Either way I'll just be working for someone else. But at least I want to get out of work on time and have weekends off. I don't have any

* All universities in China have a Communist Party branch. The party secretary is generally more powerful than the formal administrative leadership.

expectations about salary as long as I can take care of myself. I'm really in favor of avoiding marriage and kids. I'm so confused about the future, but I want to do *something*.

I Am a Leftist, and I Want to Connect with Workers

The turning point in my radicalization was encountering the left online. At first, I made online friends who were leftists and I started reading some articles. I read a class analysis piece by Fred Engst, which I thought was awesome.* I had some questions about society, but after reading this stuff I felt like I had seen the light. In my sophomore year of university, I began feeling like I was a proletarian, a worker, a regular person.

Subjectively speaking, I really identify with these terms. Growing up I rarely saw people with money, most were workers having a tough time in life and barely scraping by. When I was little, I lived in the countryside, and it was quite poor in general. My family was somewhat better off; my mom ran a restaurant, but then it went out of business. After that, things became really tough.

Things are OK now; I don't have economic demands from my family. Supporting myself shouldn't be a problem, but I'm not even considering buying a car or a house. As for "lying flat," I feel like this is an unscientific phrase.

---

* Fred Engst is the son of two leftist Americans, Erwin Engst and Joan Hinton, who moved to China in the 1940s. Fred was born and raised in China and has lived there for most of his life.

Everybody just wants to live a little better, to be a little more relaxed. Does this count as lying flat? If getting married cost less and having kids wasn't such a money pit, then the fertility rate would naturally increase. But it's not only because people can't afford to have a family. Flexible labor is a new buzzword to trick the common folk. Chairman Mao said that if the capitalist roaders take power, that will mean that capitalism has taken power and that we're doomed to perish.

I don't think people graduating this year will have an unusually hard time finding work, because it has *always* been hard. The root of high youth unemployment is capitalism. The fundamental contradiction in capitalism is between socialized production and the form of ownership. Capitalism and unemployment are two sides of the same coin. Unemployment is useful for company owners because it depresses wages and there is an always-ready reserve army. Behind the high unemployment is the system itself; it isn't created by some particular policy or enterprise. The current situation is the result of gradually accumulating contradictions.

I believe the future of China lies with the workers. I want to deeply understand workers' lives. After my internship ends, I'm planning to go get a job in a factory or connect with workers.

2
From Exams to Job Search: A Small-Town Kid Fighting Tooth and Nail

In 2022 I graduated from a top-tier university in Shandong. I didn't work much in university and I didn't go out to get training. I was in a biology education program; back then my ideal job was to be a biology teacher in middle or high school. Most of my classmates applied to graduate programs or took the public employment exam for teachers to join the system. I originally wanted to test into grad school, but I failed, so I just got a job. My grad school exam was December of last year and I didn't find work until this June. From June until now I've had two different jobs.

Xiao Yu, 2022 graduate from Henan,
worked as a tutor and lab tech

As a Teaching Assistant, I Had Lots of Complex Work but Made Little Money

Since I was an education major I was interested in joining the education sector to see if it suited me. Now I'm staying back home in a prefectural city in Henan.* It's a very small place people probably haven't heard of. Local wages aren't high; I've interviewed with a few tutoring companies. Around here it's pretty normal to have a base wage of 2,000 yuan.† I originally chose a company that is close to my house just to try it out.

When I started it was right in the middle of the busiest period of the summer courses. I took care of primary school English. Middle school classes were for teachers from the public system; they would come during the summer break to earn some extra money. I used to be a teaching assistant for them. I'd be the homeroom teacher and do various tasks including prepping class materials, printing exams, and getting the projector and presentations prepared.‡ I'd also communicate with parents, correct homework, and score exams.

This tutoring company gave me a really bad feeling and made me lose faith in the entire education and training industry. Maybe this was because they did primary and middle school and not higher grades, but it was pretty chaotic. Our department didn't have any teachers with in-class experience to manage things, we only had untrained staff who usually just communicated with the parents. They

* "Prefectural city" refers to the administrative unit directly below the provincial level.

† This refers to monthly wages. Many cities in Henan had a monthly minimum wage of 2,000 yuan (or thereabouts) in 2025.

‡ A direct translation of "homeroom teacher" is "class director." This person is responsible for administrative tasks, discipline, and communicating with parents, among other tasks, for the students under their supervision.

didn't understand pedagogy at all and were careless with the classes. Also I can't stand that I was in the office for over a month and I never sat down in my own chair. If they saw I had a tiny bit of downtime, they'd have me go supervise a class. Other teachers insisted that I go sit in on their classes. It was really annoying. I also had to watch the primary school kids while they were studying. Some parents are too busy, don't have time to watch their kids, and don't want them just playing at home all day, so they send them to the summer tutoring sessions to have them watch online cartoon classes. We're there to just watch them all day.

Primary school kids are all right, just a little noisy. The big problem is that the salary is too low. The rate for one-on-one classes with primary school kids is 120 yuan per hour, but I only earn 25 for two hours; they're really trying to get a bargain. When I tried to negotiate with them, they said I already earned the base wage and that they hadn't required me to look after too many classes per month. At the time they wouldn't sign a labor contract with me even though my colleague had one. The contract he signed required an internship of six months after which he'd get social insurance. But after he completed the six months, they fired him. Aside from particularly large or well-regulated tutoring companies, most don't provide social insurance. The month I worked there I earned the 2,000-yuan base wage, 200 for the full attendance bonus (being a homeroom teacher is a lot, but they only give 200). I had ten one-on-one classes, which was twenty hours altogether, so I did all this work in one month but only earned 2,700. Afterward, I quit right away.

There is a lot of cheap labor because it's summer break. They give the part-time university students 2,000 per month, with no other benefits, and the workload is very heavy every day. There are a lot of us female students from teacher education universities. Most female teachers are very responsible. For example, during the study periods the little kids are supposed to be watching cartoons, but they still do summer homework. So we have to help guide them. If the teachers are responsible, it's a lot of work, because you are doing one-on-one with each kid, and watching them the entire day.

But in the tutoring classes they prefer male teachers. This is because they think us women teachers speak too gently or that we won't use a loud enough voice to coax the children, so we won't be able to manage them, and the kids will be too noisy. But kids are just like this naturally; they have a lot of energy and it's impossible to have them sit all day. They'll always have those kinds of thoughts.

We got a day and a half off per week, and there was also a lot of invisible overtime.* They say it's an eight-hour day, but they required that you arrive half an hour early each day. For example, I taught a class that starts at 8 a.m., but I needed to check in using my DingTalk location at 7:30, and I'd be fined 10 yuan if I didn't.† I also wasn't allowed to go home for lunch since students eat in the school. After classes

* In English this would typically be called "unpaid overtime," but I've translated the phrase literally.

† 钉钉 in Chinese, a communication app owned by Alibaba.

ended at 6 p.m., us teachers still needed to clean the classroom, the hallways, the bathrooms, basically every person needed to take care of a classroom and hallway. There was a lot of invisible overtime, it was really taxing. Even once you've clearly finished work, if something suddenly comes up, they'll just call you. Or it could be that some parents have something to discuss; they'll give you a call. Nobody is worried that you're resting, and you can't refuse. And when our tutoring class is busy there are no fixed days off. They can move things around and will only give you a day off once it's not busy. They also don't want you to come when it's not busy because if you come, they have to pay you for the day.

There's also the issue of kids fighting, and safety issues. For example, there was this one girl who was arguing and fighting with another person, I'm not even sure why. She straight-up slapped the other person in the face and pinched her neck. Dealing with this kind of disturbance is a real pain. The boss had to go apologize to the parents, and paying this money left him out of sorts and he tried to unload the responsibility onto us. He said that if this kind of fight happened again in our class we'd have to pay, that he'd deduct our wages.

Later they wanted me to take over a lead teaching role. But I learned about the situation: If they didn't have enough students then we'd have to set up a booth on the street and pass out flyers, kind of like sales work. And you also have to do various other kinds of work; it isn't purely a teaching job. I kind of hate this. They try to make everything look pretty while increasing parents' anxiety, charging super-high class fees, while paying us hardly anything. There are so many issues, they can't stand to see us sitting there prepping class and making our presentations. I got so annoyed with the job. I didn't even get to teach. It felt so meaningless.

I have a friend who is a teaching assistant in Wenzhou, Zhejiang Province. I think things are more developed over there. They frequently share stuff with me and it seems pretty good; they play with the kids, they can study some things and also relax a little bit. But in Henan both the high school and university entrance exams are really hard. When the government attacked the tutoring industry it was pretty brutal for us.* Parents and kids weren't going to just abandon after-school tutoring. Now, the tutoring classes are really intense, they start from primary school. Our summer classes had nonstop inspections. The on-duty teacher downstairs has a button. [When inspectors come] they press the button and it will ring in the upstairs offices. Our tutoring classes were operating like this in secret. Officially, they are showing the kids cartoons to let them relax and learn. But in reality they are in class, it's still all about their grades and their ranking. I feel really bad that they're under pressure.

* In 2021, the central government launched a crackdown on private tutoring schools, impacting millions of students and teachers.

Teachers Can Be Competitive with Each Other and Untrustworthy

At first when I joined the tutoring company, I thought relationships between teachers were pretty simple, but it turned out they were quite complicated. If we're offering similar subjects, of course there will be competition. Teachers also need to do sales to recruit students. Even though we collect an introductory fee from them, the fee is quite low. For example, after the summer courses end, teachers still have to keep promoting one-on-one classes or renewals for fall classes. If I'm the homeroom teacher, then I'm pretty familiar with all the kids in the class and I communicate frequently with their parents. But if those students were brought in by another teacher there will be questions about their renewal fees: Do they belong to me or to the other person? This is one of those small money-related frictions. Then there are issues about which teacher will take which students; this causes a lot of problems here. Since they often move our rest days around, the issue of who gets to take a day off when is really complicated.

I asked one of my colleagues, who is quite capable, about her salary. She asked me to say mine first, and after I told her she said hers was the same. I just told her directly and in the moment I didn't think about it carefully. But later I thought about it more and her salary and class fees probably aren't the same as mine. She also messed with me when I left the job. My original plan was to leave at the end of the month right after our class finished its assessment and we'd corrected the exams and sorted out the grades. This way, I thought, the program might try to retain me and this would give me the upper hand. But one day I was chatting with this colleague and mentioned my plan to leave the job, and she told me that there was a rule that you needed to give advance notice. So I told the program and then in the next few days they gave me a jam-packed schedule of one-on-ones, and I couldn't just leave because then I'd lose my 200-yuan attendance bonus. I'd suffered a lot for those 200 yuan, clocking in every day. In the end I felt really unhappy. It wasn't until later that I learned she'd also wanted to leave work in August, so she was just pushing me out there to test the waters.

She was born in 2002, one year after me, and I'd always wanted to kind of look out for her. I never thought she'd treat me like this. I think it's because she knew the rules inside and out. She's a local and did her undergrad here. This is a small place, and she has more personal connections here. Also, when she was in university she had always been a class cadre and so is pretty familiar with those rules;* she really knows how to deal with parents and kids. Her one-on-ones are always full, and she has a lot of student resources. She is super competent and handles her work easily. It seems like she is good at negotiating, including over wages. But when I wanted to negotiate, management declined and said everyone gets the same thing. They said if they gave me a raise they'd have to give others a raise. The company tries to see who is easier to handle.

* Class cadre is a kind of leadership role for students, involving various supervisory tasks.

Grads from Elite Universities Have Advantages, but Even for Them, Small Cities Offer Limited Employment Opportunities

When I stopped working at the tutoring company, I started to look for work online. I put my résumé up on Boss and submitted it all over but basically didn't hear back.* Since I was a biology major I looked for pharmaceutical companies. After I quit my previous job I had three or four days off, then I started at a pharmaceutical company. I wanted to do microbiological testing, but they wouldn't let me. They sent me to physiochemical testing to assess whether the ingredients in the medicines were up to standard.

It's relatively easy for people with my major to find work. Also, this is a small town, and my degree is from a top-tier university, so it's relatively easy. But I applied to lots of other industries—either they didn't look at my messages at all, or they did and never replied. Not even customer service would get back to me.

It felt like some of the companies were trying to trick people. For example, I had an interview with a company that seemed pretty legit; the whole interview process felt decent. At first, I thought they did sales, but when I asked for more details about the job, it turned out they did debt collection for a bank.

My mom got sick and had to be hospitalized this June, so I was mostly focused on picking a job close to home. But our little county town actually doesn't have any good jobs.

* Boss is an online employment portal.

I have a bachelor's degree and I thought I'd be able to get any job, but it didn't feel that way when I was applying. If the position wasn't directly connected to my major, to teaching or to biology, then I had a really hard time. Otherwise I could work as a cashier in a supermarket, that type of mostly physical labor with long hours and no skill requirements, things that anybody can do.

Of course, my degree is helpful. Some of my colleagues from the tutoring company didn't get as many students as me, maybe because their degree wasn't quite as good as mine. The company really trusted me as soon as I started working there and right away gave me one-on-one classes. At the second biopharmaceutical company I worked at, I chatted with other colleagues and learned that our salaries were different; because we had different degrees, they earned 200 to 500 yuan less. I earned about 1,000 less than people with graduate degrees.

They still really care about degrees; having a degree improves the job search. I have a local friend who graduated from a professional college, and it has been really hard for them to find work.* They got a job frying and selling baozi for breakfast. It's so exhausting and now the weather is so hot. They did it for a little while and then quit.

A colleague of mine who worked at the tutoring company for six months and then quit had a hard time finding a new job because she was an English major. She had been thinking about switching to doing e-commerce. But her mom wouldn't let her, she said that kind of work didn't require

* "Professional college" appears in the original as 专科.

any skill. She said, “Even someone like me can do that, you’re educated and shouldn’t be doing that kind of work.” She hoped her daughter could find work as a teacher. So she went back to looking for tutoring work and found a job, but the base wage was only 1,800, and they didn’t give any class fees. Her family thought that since she’d only graduated this year, she should take the job; at least she’d get some experience. They wanted her to work and prepare to take the public employment or civil service exams.

The cost of living in our little county town is low. (The wages are also low.) As a university graduate, I can earn 3,000 a month. But within the state system, like the tobacco bureau, you can make 7,000 to 8,000. And you don’t have to work hard; if you’re taking a nap there in the evening that still counts as overtime, and you’ll still get bonus pay. So everyone wants to work at those kinds of places. Personal connections are super important in small towns, it’s the same for teachers and civil servants. In small towns you really rely on personal connections and information. In my pharmaceutical company some colleagues were also introduced to the company via personal connections.

Management at My New Job Is Deceptive, but the Company Doesn’t Force Employees to Do Overtime

Since coming to the pharmaceutical company, I start work at 8:30 a.m., get a break from 11:30 to 1:30, and then work till 5:30 in the afternoon. It’s an hour less per day than my previous job, but I definitely feel like it is more physically taxing. I have to do lab trials and testing while walking back and forth to various rooms. I also have to write reports by hand. At the tutoring company I'd finish class every hour so there were fixed breaks. But now, when we're busy I might have to go the whole morning or afternoon without even having time to get a drink of water.

I'm still in the internship phase and am making 3,000 per month. The pay is so low. But usually I don't have to work overtime; my colleagues have held on to the principle of not doing overtime. As soon as it hits 5:30 they're out of here, since management won't force you to work overtime. The leaders will complain sometimes, but at least when it comes to overtime, they mostly understand our perspective. For example, I live about a thirty-minute ride away by e-bike. If I had to work overtime I wouldn't get home until really late, and as a woman I wouldn't feel safe. So, they won't force me to work overtime and usually there are no issues.

Our leader is a guy in his thirties or forties. When I started the job, management used all kinds of emotionally manipulative tactics. At the time I wanted to do microbiological testing, but they kept insisting that it wasn't a good fit for my major. Actually it was just that they didn't have enough people to do physiochemical testing. A lot of people had quit and they couldn't replace them, so they put me in that role.

All the Workers Are Pissed Off About Fines, and a Wave of People Have Voted with Their Feet

Why doesn't this department have enough people? There's a lot to be said here! According to my colleagues, the company wanted to start a partnership with a Korean company back in June of this year. The Koreans had sent a team here to do an inspection to check out the company, to see if the testing standards were up to speed. My colleagues did a lot of prep and were really busy; they had to do overtime, but in the end they didn't pass the inspection. Then the company deducted 1,000 yuan from each person's paycheck. They also didn't get the normal 3,000–4,000 yuan holiday bonus, so altogether everyone lost around 5,000. One employee who had been there for over a year couldn't contain their anger and quit on the spot. With that, a pillar of the department was gone.

People in other teams grumbled but they didn't have any way to stop the wage deductions. They were upset that they'd had their money stolen, but all they could do was leave and forget about trying to wrangle with the company. The reports from the Korean company were given to our company in 2021, but the employees from 2021 had already left. The group that was there in June of this year was different; they hadn't written the report but they suffered the consequences. We were all afraid because we had heard a group would be coming from the EU in December to do an inspection, so we were worried that there would be more wage deductions then.

If I was fined 1,000 yuan I would also quit straight away; forget about the holiday bonus. I wouldn't take any legal actions: My head hurts just thinking about that whole process because I feel like the time and energy would not be worth the result.

Sexual Harassment Demands a Legal Response

Some of my colleagues at the pharmaceutical company have dealt with sexual harassment. When they started working, the boss straight up checked out their body, their appearance, and then forced some of them to go drinking with him. One colleague had to go out all night to eat and drink with customers, and the boss didn't look after her. This person used to work in digital media, and she had dealt with this kind of stuff before.

It's best to try to avoid whatever you can in the moment. My colleague decided not to get dressed up, so her boss wouldn't notice her. She's not that keen about dressing up, so it was easy for her to give it up.

I haven't actually looked into what kinds of legal options or ways to complain there are. I was also badly deceived by the tutoring company I worked at. When I interviewed, they told me the base wage was 2,500, but after I joined it became 2,000. I didn't have any evidence and hadn't thought to record the interview or anything; they always called me to discuss things, and I didn't have anything in writing. So I had to admit defeat.

Wage deductions are one thing, but sexual harassment and "unwritten rules" demand a legal response.* We can't let these kinds of things slide.

---

* 潜规则 (translated as "unwritten rules"), here presumably referring to the expectation that women will accompany their male superiors in the evening if asked.

Data Gets Fabricated, and the Workplace Is Unsafe

There are some problems with the work we do: We fabricate data. For instance, if our tests of a medicine don't produce any results, management will tell us to make something up. When we're writing up reports we need numbers; how much of a sample is being weighed, for example. These need to be printed out, and then we need to document the final results and the way they were calculated. The printed labels have to include the calculation process, the date, and signatures of the person who did the inspection and the person who verified it. But for some samples, for example if you can't get a read on the moisture, management will tell us to make something up that is within a reasonable range. In some of these small instances they'll just fabricate things. They will test for bigger issues, but they won't be happy if the tests come back and the sample isn't up to standard. They'll say, "How could this have such a big error?" and they'll hold the inspector responsible.

I encounter a lot of reagents in my current job and there aren't adequate precautionary measures. Some of these reagents are carcinogenic. But the company doesn't give us any subsidies, and their public position is that employees are there of their own free will. I'm dealing with these dangerous carcinogens every day at work.

The internship period at this pharmaceutical company is three months. I'm thinking about not transferring to a permanent position; after getting some experience here I want to jump ship to another company. My mom's health is OK now and I can go a bit farther away; I don't absolutely have to stay in this little town of ours. Companies are really poorly regulated in these small towns.

My Brother Is Having a Rough Time with Work and There's Little Family Support

I have an older brother. I was born in 2001, right at the end of the family planning policy, and my family was fined more than 10,000 yuan. They didn't have any money to begin with, and back then 10,000 was a lot of money. The character for my name is related to "being fined."

It's tough to find work now, but since I have a degree I can find something in this little town if I really want to. I'm not satisfied with the job I have now, and it doesn't pay well, but at least I can do it. But my brother is a high school grad and has had a terrible time looking for work.

He used to work in an auto-parts plant in Foshan, Guangdong Province. The conditions were quite good there and he liked the job; with overtime he could earn 7,000 to 8,000 a month. Originally it was a Japanese auto plant, and while it was Japanese owned the conditions were very good. When it was hot inside workers would get a subsidy, and they'd get gift cards for holidays. They had plenty of the items they needed each day, like gloves and stuff like that. But later, when the gas-powered car industry wasn't doing well and the Japanese company pulled their investment, it became a Taiwanese joint venture.* After the

---

* While it's not stated, the implication is that this is a Taiwanese-Chinese joint venture.

Taiwanese came in, the conditions in the factory started getting worse, and then they started layoffs. He was laid off in October of last year during the pandemic.

After that he was looking for work nonstop, but didn't find anything as good as his previous job. He would do some super casual jobs like home renovations and that kind of physical labor.

His old job in the Foshan factory provided him with social insurance. When he lost his job, he got three months of unemployment payments. Even though it wasn't a lot of money, at least he had a bit each month. Since coming back home he hasn't had coverage because he has to pay around 2,000 per month for his mortgage.

Now he can't find any work at all; he's just staying at home feeling anxious. It was raining here, his car was parked outside and it got flooded. It had to be brought in for repairs, and he was in a terrible mood. After that he went straight home.

When I have problems at work I don't tell my family about them. I might say a few words to my brother, but I don't tell him about really troubling things. I usually complain to my friends or colleagues, I don't say much to my family. They really want to help me, but they don't have any resources, so I have to look for work myself. When I've found work, I'll mention more or less what's happening, but when I'm worried while looking for work I won't say anything to them. If I tell them, they'll be worried and then blame themselves for not having the capacity to help, so I think not saying anything is best.

For Small-Town Kids, the Only Way to Succeed Is to Get Good Grades

I think much of involution is unnecessary, like chasing grades. I am licensed to be a high school teacher, so why haven't I gone on to be a high school teacher in the public system? It's because I had such a bad experience in high school. I was really depressed for all of high school, I didn't know what I was doing day-to-day. Every day felt really difficult, math and physics were so difficult, I felt like I just couldn't do it. I was so depressed through high school, when I think about going to be a high school teacher I feel like I can't stand the oppression of taking the university entrance exam. So, I think that primary or middle school would be a bit better for me, but the oppression of high school has already extended down to middle and primary schools. Now in middle schools it's really hard for students to pass the high school entrance exam.

I think they could establish Shanhe University; even if it doesn't actually exist you could have it online.* After all, the internet is so developed these days, university students basically all know how to use it. Mostly it's because those of us in these four provinces [Shandong, Shanxi, Hebei, Henan] are so disadvantaged, there aren't any universities. Otherwise these students wouldn't be so miserable. In

---

* Shanhe is a fictional university created by netizens. It's a portmanteau word combining Shanxi, Shandong, Henan, and Hebei, four provinces that lack resources in higher education but have a lot of students.

Henan, we only have one 211 school, Zhengzhou University.*
All the others are pretty mediocre.

The university entrance exam is a filter; each place is unequal. There is educational inequality, everyone has somewhat different exams, and different places have different qualifying scores. For example, if you're a Shanghai local then it might be very easy for you to get into Fudan, but for us we need to work so hard to get accepted.† To begin with, they're in a big city, we're already far behind them, and then getting into these schools is easier for them.

Everybody knows they have to study as this is the only way to overcome your place of birth. My family is from the countryside—this is the only path out for me. If I hadn't studied and just went out to get a job, I probably wouldn't succeed because people still care about your degree. My friend from primary school is already married. If my grades hadn't been good back then, I'd be doing the same.

Her husband's family is all right, but who knows exactly what her life will be like, especially after they have kids. I think getting married is fine, but having kids is a whole pile of trouble. I have a cousin who went out to get a job right around when she finished middle school. Her mom was worried and left with her. After she worked away from home for a couple of years, her family arranged a match for her and she got married. She had two boys; the younger one

* The number 211 refers to a group of relatively elite universities that received central government support as part of a plan to improve higher education.

† One of the top schools in China, located in Shanghai.

is now two years old. When I see her life, it is not my ideal. Even though she has a house and a car, having a house and a car doesn't mean you're doing well in life. After you have kids, you have to keep worrying about their education. It's like you didn't have the ability to escape [by studying] and now you have to worry about your kids getting out all over again. Education and grade involution just keeps happening.

I don't have any plans to have kids, and my big brother is ahead of me. He's twelve years older, already over thirty and he hasn't even gotten married. So he's bearing the pressure from the entire family, and I'm just like whatever, nobody is pressuring me. He doesn't have any plans to get married and have kids. The family gives him pressure, like they pressure him to take out a loan to buy a house, but they can't force him to accept matches.

Universities Are Continuously Expanding Enrollment, but Students' Future Employment Prospects Are Uncertain

Why is there youth unemployment? As an example: Our school does teacher education, and it recruits more and more students each year. Our class is twice as big as the last one, and the one after us is twice as big as ours. I think that there has been a gradual decline in demand for teachers. With the birth rate we have now, of course there will be less demand for teachers in the future; some schools will even have to close. Some day cares are already unable to continue because they can't get students. But our program is continuously expanding enrollment, and our curriculum is really messy and chaotic. This is not helpful for us if we have to change to a different line of work; they're trapping so many people. The configuration of this major is unreasonable. The university might be expanding enrollment just so it can stay afloat.

But from a broader perspective, I feel like I don't even know what to say. Definitely there are problems with specific policies; the university entrance exam has already been denounced for so long.

As for testing into grad school, in the third year of our education major, classes are already completed. So aside from your studies, in that period you start preparing for the exam. Grad school exam prep has already involuted down to year two. The chain businesses near our school are really thriving, including those dorms for grad-exam tutoring. There are some people who hear about the reputation of our school, so they want to study and live nearby. Before the pandemic you didn't have to scan your face to come into the school, and there were students from other places coming in. But they started being stricter after the pandemic and now we need to scan our face to get in; it seems like other people can't enter. It's so crazy and there are no opportunities for entertainment or activities, everybody just studies. It's impossible to see an alternative path, there's no choice.

My Employer's Pandemic Lockdown Policy Was Unreasonable, and After I Was Released, I Missed the Grad School Entrance Exam Because I Had a Fever

Although I was forced to take the university entrance exam, and forced to compete, my complaints were about problems with the education system. I thought the exam system was fair and it even gave me an opportunity. But the pandemic was really a blow; we were on lockdown in our school for six months. At that time I had just found a part-time job at a tutoring company where the money was pretty good, 50 yuan per hour, and it felt pretty relaxing. The class was following the format set up by a foreign teacher. After the foreign teacher left, they hired university students like us to run the class. Each class period we'd teach students a few words, we'd study and play at the same time, and we'd do some simple and fun games with them. We had everything worked out, but then I was put on lockdown on campus. Our school's management policies were really unreasonable. We couldn't leave the dorm and we had to line up every day to get a PCR test. I thought everything was so meaningless.

During the pandemic we complained online. But they would search for these posts and would even come looking for individuals.* Then your advisor would come to have a chat and get you to delete the post. I'm not sure how they went about figuring out who posted what, maybe they

* "They" is not specified here, but it seems to refer to school authorities.

checked the Weibo account number; everyone posted in the Weibo Super Topics section.*

They eventually let us out, right? I was still pretty miserable after we were released, and right on the first day of the grad school entrance exam I got a fever. When I went to the hospital to have my blood drawn, I almost fainted. I was so swollen I felt like I couldn't breathe. I don't know if it was from fear or what, and then when I got a fever my body was pretty frail. I felt like I just couldn't catch my breath and that I was close to death. The color in my face was not right. I was unable to breathe, and my face had started turning colors, so I went to the emergency room. In the ER there were people everywhere and not enough beds. Some people were suffering but couldn't see a doctor and just lay down in the hallways. It was so chaotic.

In the ER they said I didn't have a high fever so they wouldn't give me fever-reducing medicine. My fever didn't come down at all that day. Maybe the hospital didn't have any medicine that day; they wouldn't give you anything unless your fever hit 38.5°C [101.3°F]. There was no medicine for sale, but my brother managed to get some from his friend who had extra. They gave me two boxes of ibuprofen.

After going through all of this it felt like things had gone too far. They didn't have to do all these things, especially the PCR tests and the dorm lockdowns. When they locked us up, I felt like I was going to have emotional problems

---

* 微博超话.

and was so anxious every day. Bringing it up today, I still feel wounded.

Lab Techs Are Undervalued; My Future Seems Full of Choices, but I Feel Lost

In this job I get so annoyed when I'm repeatedly asked to fabricate the data, or when the tests come back in error, that I will think about quitting. But for the moment, I don't think I have any better options. I only have to work seven hours a day, there isn't overtime, and the wages are OK for this area. I'm always looking for work, but it seems like I won't find anything with better conditions.

I've considered going to work at a biotech company in Suzhou, but I've heard that overtime is really bad over there. I've also thought about going to Beijing, or somewhere in the south like Guangzhou or Shenzhen. As for the salaries, it depends on local living expenses. I actually don't have a particular standard in mind, but I'm sure it's more expensive than here. And biotech companies are usually pretty far from the city center, so rent shouldn't be too expensive.

I still really need to work. I was so anxious when I was out of work, I felt like I didn't have anything to do. When I have a job, I feel like each day will be fulfilling. Even if I leave this job, I will keep looking for work. I won't stay at home being unemployed. My family doesn't have the means to keep supporting me. I think that even if they had the means, I would still want to go out and work. I really like the environment at home but now that I'm grown up I hope to have my own space to exist more independently. I still really depend on my family. I haven't yet had the experience of living on my own: renting a house, eating, and working independently. I've been living at my aunt's house all along, and she gave me my e-bike. So at least I don't have any issues with housing or things like that.

The advantage of working close to home is that it's easy to get together with friends since they all live nearby. For instance, I got to be friends with one of my colleagues from the tutoring school. The pharmaceutical company I work at now is only four minutes from where she lives. Sometimes I don't want to ride my e-bike home in the evening, so I just go to her house to sleep. In the middle of the day, I get off at 11:30 a.m. and she's off at noon. If we both want to take a break I go back to her place and prepare the food first and when she gets back we eat together. After we eat, she cleans up and then we can have a little rest. This is really great.

The employment options for people in my major are to work as a teacher or join a biotech company, and I've tried both. I've thought about changing professions in the future, but I'd need to learn more first. I haven't made up my mind; right now I'm working and considering it at the same time, but I haven't seen any opportunities. If you're going to change professions, shouldn't your point of departure be your own interests and strengths? But I don't have any particular strengths. I was totally wrecked by high school education, and I don't have any special talents. So, I hope I can just be a little happy each day and study some things that interest me and then develop in that direction. I know it's a bit vague, but it's because I still haven't figured out my interests.

I don't have to work too much now so I have some time to myself in the evenings. I get home each night by 6:30 p.m. and then I have my own time, it's pretty nice. My hobby now is reading, because I always wanted to read books before but didn't have the resources to buy them. I read all kinds of things; I'm interested in popular science and novels. I even bought a used Kindle so I can download e-books, and each month I read up to five books.

I used to be obsessed with video games, but I don't really play anymore. I want to discover more things that interest me and study some new topics. I'm interested in computers and have been reading about this recently. I've tried it out a bit just to see if I'm a good fit or not, even though I've heard that there is a lot of involution for people doing this kind of work. I just wanted to give programming a shot, but I don't know if I'll try to go in this direction.

Schools Have Limited Support for Job Searches, and Falsify Their Graduates' Employment Statistics

When I graduated, the school provided a little bit of support in my job search. My school is in Shandong; they mostly have connections with local jobs within the province. My classmates from Shandong got more help, but this wasn't useful for me because I didn't want to stay in that area. That was during the pandemic so there was only online recruitment; the appropriate procedures were still in place. Most of the positions were in education, either in schools or tutoring companies. There weren't as many in biotech companies, but some held info sessions. Local schools would all come to us to recruit for positions in the public system. Our school is highly regarded in Shandong, so if recruits can pass an interview, they don't need to take an exam. Then they can go directly to working in the school, in the public employment system.

As for the government, how do I put it? I feel like it hasn't done anything to help me. There is no practical help, every day they send ads saying we need to develop our talents, blah-blah-blah, and look for work. There is no concrete help.

For my graduating class, basically the people going to grad school are considered to be continuing with their education, and those that get public employment have a clear path forward. But people like me who didn't get into grad school and didn't immediately find work are coerced by the school into signing a form that allows them to inflate their graduates' employment rates.* I'm not exactly clear on what it is, but if you don't sign it then your advisor will come have a chat with you. If you still refuse to sign then they use other ways of threatening you, like saying that you won't be able to graduate.

The majority of my classmates have gone to grad school and now they're studying. Some didn't get in the first year, so they tried again the following year. Some got a job in the

* Universities have been under pressure from the government to ensure employment for their graduates. There have been many reports of universities using unscrupulous approaches to inflate their employment stats.

intervening year; since we are trained as teachers, basically all of them got work that had something to do with education. It could be helping children with reading, doing crafts, or things like that. The other classmates in my circle have already gone into the public system and are high school teachers. There isn't anyone else wandering around like me.

3

Doing Odd Jobs and Paying for Myself: A Two-Pronged Plan for Employment

I studied journalism as an undergrad, and now I'm in a three-year graduate degree program also in journalism. I live in Q City [a second-tier city in the south]. *I will graduate in 2024 and am now doing an internship. Fall recruitment is about to start and I'm getting ready to look for work.*

2024 graduate of a university in Jiangnan; interning during their master's degree in journalism

Starting Out with Odd Jobs

I started doing internships every year from my sophomore year in university. My first internship was recording and editing work with a streaming platform. I'd go with my classmate to look for content and then record interviews. We left this internship after one month. Our teacher was advising more than ten people and they just didn't have the energy. So we had to go out on the street by ourselves to see what kinds of social events might attract people. Or we'd go online to Douyin to see who was posting interesting stuff, then get in touch with them and go do an interview. It was really hard to meet the requirements and we couldn't produce anything, so we left.

When I went out on the street to see if there were any interesting things happening, I wouldn't get any wages. They would only pay once you had submitted something; one video would get you 200 yuan, but that's it. I had to pay all the expenses for making the video.

In my junior year I also did video editing, but for a TV station. This internship was because I had already tested into the graduate program, and I wanted to take advantage of the winter break to get an internship because our school requires them. People from home used their personal connections to get me into the local TV station, and I did video editing for them. I felt quite clearly that overtime wasn't too bad in this kind of TV station; after editing that day's news I could go home.

After graduation, I went to work at an internet company doing digital media operations. At first, I was really looking forward to it because I had found it on my own using recruitment software, and it is a well-known internet company. But after I started, I was actually in a secondary unit that did real estate–related business. When I applied, they didn't clearly explain what department I would be in or the content of the work. Since I don't have much experience, I didn't ask enough questions in the interview. Doing content creation doesn't require you to write much of your own stuff, a lot comes from searching and curating things on the internet. Another thing that was quite different from what I imagined was that we did copy and paste work for an entire month. Every day was the repetitive task of entering property listings. I really didn't have enough experience then. I thought that I had finally gotten into an internet company—they said it was under the flag of a famous company—and I'd be doing real estate media. But we actually didn't have to write anything, basically it was just organizing information and copying and pasting.

In my first year in grad school I interned at a newspaper in Q City. When I started, they also had me do a month of work that had nothing to do with my major; it was just random tasks that required no skill at all, lots of copying and pasting. I was really falling apart then. Someone at the company told me I could tell my boss if I wanted to do something different. One month after I talked to him, he gradually started to give me some writing and interviewing tasks, so there were some changes and at least I spoke my mind. When I first started, he asked me how long I'd intern for, and I told him two months. He knew that I would probably leave after two months so maybe he didn't want to give me too much responsibility. Even though this internship was in Q City, I still had to rent an apartment and pay for my meals. I had to cover all my daily expenses, so I spent a lot of money over the summer break.

I've always done language-oriented internships, this one at the newspaper and the previous one doing content creation for a public account. Along with the TV station internship I did as an undergrad, these are all connected to my major. The internships at the TV station and newspaper were unpaid. When I was an undergrad, a lot of classmates were willing to take unpaid internships. But now that we're grad students, everyone says that they can't keep doing it "for the love," and that they need to find a paid internship. If your résumé only has some on-campus activities, it's hard to attract HR. With campus recruitment they'll prioritize student cadres, which is a way for them to tell you they expect this kind of experience. I haven't served as a cadre as a grad student, but if I get an internship and get some experience with writing, this will help me with the job search. After having done internships, I should also have a better idea of the kind of job I want since I've spent time in some companies.

I think that undergrad internships are about broadening horizons in order to understand this industry and this area. But with grad school internships, I want to join the real world while also improving myself in a certain area rather than being scattered in various directions.

Students Pay for Internships During Undergrad and Grad School

When I started my third year of grad school, in about March or April, I really wanted to find an internship to lay the groundwork and accumulate a portfolio for my future professional development. I've usually applied for something related to software or public social media accounts, because my friends and I don't know how to expand our channels for searching for internships and jobs. I looked for internships for all of March, April, and May. I don't like the things I've found, since I don't want to do an internship that won't even cover basic daily expenses. When I was an undergrad and in my first two years of grad school, I spent a lot of money doing internships. At first, I wanted to find work in a different province, something related to my major, like being a content creator. But in other provinces you usually get 100 or 120 yuan per day; it's probably not enough to cover rent and daily expenses so I'd still be losing money. I don't want to pay when I should be earning. Later a classmate sent me some info about a company, so I went for an interview. I started work there around June 20.

The salary at this job isn't that high—just 120 yuan per day—but they have employee housing. And it's also in Q City close to my school, so I ended up taking the internship.

Originally, I thought that if this company would give me a full-time position, I would take it. The content of the work and the environment aren't bad. But now I'm worried about the future of the company. It hasn't been around for long, and it's hard to survive. I've thought about it, and it seems unlikely I'll have a chance to stay here, because it seems like they only need a capable intern, not a full-time employee. I'll still have to find work for myself later.

A couple of days ago HR told my classmate and me that there is a chance to stay here, but he also said we need a backup plan because they won't be sure if it will be possible until the spring of next year. Maybe this is because they want to reduce expenses. Interns don't do any less work than regular employees but their wages are a lot lower. They tell us that there might be an opportunity to stay just to get us to keep working hard. But HR told us to have a backup plan and that we can take sick days to join the university's fall recruitment. I'm not too certain about this research institute. Those people that are regular employees have an exit strategy; they might take the civil service exam. As soon as I started here, a colleague that I have a pretty good relationship with asked me if I was planning on staying. After we had been chatting for a week, she told me that she's planning on ditching. She even used the company's printer to print out her exam certification, and HR saw her do it.*

It's really hard to recruit people in our province. We're in the same office as HR and we hear them talking about it every day. We have a PhD working here, but as far as I know this person is going to leave for a university; they're just here in a transitional phase. Our development isn't good, it probably has to do with the leaders. It's the startup phase, of course there will be difficulties and problems, this is understandable. My manager said that you'll encounter various kinds of intrigue when you go out into the real world. He told me to just do my job and not to take sides, just look after my own interest.

I Want Work and I Want to Live

I have to do overtime at my current internship, and they've called us to work on the weekend many times. Recently I've felt like our leaders have become manipulative. My manager asked me to write an article, and after just said,

---

* Referring to the civil service exam.

"it's hard work": just those words, "it's hard work."* Recently the upper management held a meeting and said that the company has to reduce costs. My manager said a lot of employees have been doing overtime for no reason and that he saw me doing overtime on the weekend but that I hadn't submitted an overtime application. He's encouraging us to do overtime but not to do the overtime application. I've just started the internship, and he wants me to do even more work.

Everyone does overtime. It seems like interns don't submit overtime applications, but regular employees do. Maybe interns are too embarrassed to do it. We don't even have to talk to our managers, it can be done through an online system, but we're still embarrassed. Among regular employees, each person has a different view of whether to submit the paperwork; my manager doesn't do it. Our publicity work is just like this, we don't know when we'll suddenly have to send something out, and my manager said he's already used to this kind of [unpaid] overtime.

As a journalist I go out during the day to do interviews and then write up the article. In the evening, I edit the article because the editor needs to do the layout at night. If he has any questions, he'll call over and we'll go through it together. I can deal with this, and I'm even willing to do more because I want to learn to be better. But I also want to say, I can do more but I still want my own life. I want work and I want to live.

---

* The implication is that the speaker wanted more recognition of their contribution.

My earlier internships were all for two months; I didn't really integrate into those groups. Since the company thinks that I'm just an intern for two months, they won't be that patient in training me or see me as my own person. This is how I feel anyway. But my current internship is the most comfortable I've felt in one of these jobs. When I was interviewing a while back, they said the internship would be rather long and they believed I could stay for a while, so they started to gradually train me. My manager thinks of me as a little sister and has been training me. He doesn't think that just because I'm an intern I'm not part of this research institute, and I appreciate that.

Involution isn't so serious in our company. We can't always leave work right on time, but if you have to leave it seems like nobody will say anything about it. For now, I can handle a job that is rather "involuted" or demands overtime. I want to take advantage of this moment when I'm still young and just getting out into the world to improve myself and expand my skills; this way I'll have more options later. But I'm always seeing online how if you're too overworked when you're young it will lead to some kind of health stuff. Maybe I'm up for doing a bit more work, as long as it doesn't harm my body. If my health is bad, then later on I'll have to give all my money to the hospital.

Our school hasn't said anything about labor laws, I don't know if they'll say more about them during the fall recruitment season. Those classmates of mine that have already graduated have told me that if I want to work within this province their wages are around 6,000 or 7,000 with housing provided. This is more or less what it's like in Q City.

I've gradually accepted that if I stay in the province my wages will be about like this, because Q City is just at this level. If I can find a job in a different province and I like the content of the work and the wages are acceptable, I'd really like to go for it. But most of my classmates stay in Q City. Maybe I'll be just like everyone else and stay here.

There Are Many Causes of High Youth Unemployment, but We Can Only Control Ourselves

I think there are a lot of reasons for high youth unemployment. A lot of factors including the pandemic, economic conditions, and others that we just can't control. The only thing we can control is ourselves, like our own specialization and abilities. In our major, so many people are taking the civil service exam rather than becoming journalists because if one hasn't developed their skills in this area of specialization [journalism] there actually aren't many jobs one can do.

We receive training from traditional journalists, focusing on things like interviewing, writing, editing, and layout. People in our major really want to join a famous internet company, but we only get pretty superficial training from the school in things like Photoshop or Premiere. If we want to learn these things we still have to join a club or do it on our own outside of class. But if I hadn't joined these clubs it would have been hard to do it on my own. Mostly people haven't thought about what they're going to do later. I joined a club back in sophomore year, so I have a bit of a foundation.

I feel like nobody in my major is really lying flat. Even if they aren't particularly focused, everyone has their own ideas and approximate direction. None of us are really putting in a lot of effort to look for jobs yet. So I don't think we count as lying flat. We haven't even graduated, we're still gradually joining the real world, but it's like we're being forced to participate in involution. If you don't have experience with internships then it's really hard to find work. Isn't taking the civil service exam just like this? They're only going to take one person, it's not that other people aren't qualified, it's just that there aren't the resources. So some people just keep taking the exams over and over again.

Everything Revolves Around the State System

One of my classmates is in a trial period in a government job. It's nine to five, and she's always telling me about how leisurely her day-to-day is. Every day when I'm sitting down to work, she's telling me that people in her office haven't even arrived yet. She graduated in the first half of the year. She was constantly taking exams to try to get a position in the public system but couldn't succeed. Later she applied for some talent recruitment programs in the southeast but didn't get anything. Lots of positions were only hiring one person and she would be the runner-up. Now that she's found this trial position in the government, she's planning to take the exam there next year.

Today she was also trying to convince me to take the civil service exam. I'm really anxious about this right now.

I need to take care of my internship work but also deal with the job search, and then my advisor will ask about my thesis from time to time. I feel like I'm failing trying to do all three things all at once. We work from 8:30 a.m. to 5:30 p.m., with an hour and a half for lunch. If I'm going to take the civil service exam I need to watch test-prep videos, but I don't have much time to study after I get off from work. Lots of my classmates haven't gotten internships; they're fully devoting themselves to studying for the civil service exam. Among the graduates, there are usually fewer than ten who can pass the exam. But 80 or 90 percent of people take the exam; the success rate is too low. Too many people are applying for a single position and you can't land the position unless you get the top score. I think that it totally isn't that people don't have the skills for the job, but just that there are too many people; everyone's trying to squeeze onto the same path.

I know that to prep for the written exam people watch things online and read various materials. To prep for the interview, they might enroll in a class, those kinds of two- or three-day courses that guarantee success. If you succeed, they get to keep your money. If you don't pass, they also might not return your money; it's a gamble. I think the companies are also gambling because they charge 2,000 to 4,000 yuan per week. With so many people enrolling in the course, there will always be a few people who pass the interview. The companies always make money; they won't suffer a loss. I also think that they can't help you improve your interview skills that much, it's completely not worth that much money. But maybe some people think that if you don't pass they'll return your fees, and if you do pass you won't get your money back but you've made it into the system, so it's a good outcome. A lot of people have this attitude when they enroll in these courses. The past few years these exam-prep companies have made a ton of money.

My dad, mom, and sister are all urging me to take the civil service exam. My parents' view is that I've gotten a master's degree, I've done all this schooling: If I go out and just work for a company, has all that education been a waste?

I thought about going straight to graduate study when I was an undergrad. Originally, I was in a non-elite school, then as an undergraduate I wanted to enter the system, so I picked a 211 university, it wasn't that hard.* Then I decided I would go straight to grad school. I hadn't thought that there would be so many people trying to take the civil service exam; I was surprised that my classmates were thinking about the exam as soon as they started their studies. When I started my studies, I still had some ideals about journalism and thought that I would work in media. After I had some internships, these ideas began to gradually disappear.

I abandoned looking for work that is related to my journalism major. I don't want to be a journalist, but I do want to write things, I've always wanted to write and accumulate some of my own works. But to be honest, when I've been in internships, they aren't very relevant. Lots are looking for

* "Non-elite school" is 双非的学校.

people who know certain software; usually they are looking for social media, content creation, or copy for platforms. Finding internships has been really difficult. I knew what the content of the work would be like for this job when I interviewed. They told me I'd be writing these things; it's well-matched for my professional development plan.

As an undergrad and grad student I did journalism internships. Every time I joined a new workplace the people who worked there would advise me to get out. Journalists aren't doing as well as before. News media is a public institution, but now it's been corporatized. Their work is exhausting, and they have to constantly write articles since wages are based on the number of articles they write. If you aren't working hard to write articles then your salary will be lower, so they're under a lot of pressure. When I did an internship at *Q City Daily* it felt like the journalists didn't have any status, they just had to serve everyone else. It felt like they were begging people to take an interview, and often they'd be turned down or ignored, even though interviews are an opportunity for publicity. Journalists need to continuously communicate with others and constantly double-check details; the whole process seems really exhausting.

But the past few days I've been thinking about my professional plans. I think that if I really can't find other work then I can be a journalist. Those of us in the liberal arts don't have sharp boundaries between the majors, if I want to go find other kinds of work, I won't find anything. Being a journalist isn't my top choice, but I will do it, I won't fight it. Location isn't that important for me, I'm more concerned with the work content.

Now I'm more interested in finding a job with content that I like, and one that fits my personality. I don't want something that is super challenging, because it will consume me from within.

My undergrad professor said that after five years there would be fewer than five of us working as journalists [. . .] Some have done pretty well and are working for leading media outlets within China. But I feel like grad students are more conservative and tend toward taking the civil service exams. There are only two of us who are journalists, it's so few. It seems like some people decided they wanted to be civil servants even before they started grad school. When I had just graduated, I think I still had some journalism ideals, but after doing grad school I've been considering other things. Being a journalist, I've seen too much; I won't choose this job.

I'm really confused by grad students' thinking. Why is everyone so obsessed with taking the civil service exam? My family is the same way. This has given me some anxiety, because I don't have much time now to study for the exam. And also, I don't really like that kind of life inside the system. My parents have their perspective and just give their advice. I usually make decisions about my own things and don't really discuss much with them. I've made my own decisions since I was young. If I discuss something with them, they don't really understand me. The last time I shared my thoughts about work with them they said I definitely have to take the civil service exam, that I *have* to do it. It made me pretty angry.

The kind of family pressure I'm talking about are those traditional family values. I'm afraid that if I enter the system, things will change, that I'll have to take the road of traditional families.

Life within the system might be like my classmate said. There is more leisure time and then you can start to get married, have kids, support your husband, and educate the children. If I join the system, I'm afraid the system will give me this kind of family pressure. The social environment there will put me on the road to a traditional family.

Women Are More Likely to Face Employment Discrimination

Last year when we were looking for work, one of my classmates told me that she felt obvious employment discrimination and found that companies preferred men. She is a journalism and communications major and graduated two years ago. She was looking for a related job and, all else being equal, men were accepted first. My classmate gave me some professional advice, saying that in our province it was super easy for men with master's degrees from a 211 university to get a job. There have always been more women in our major, but employers hoped to be able to hire men. So not only are there more women, but the competition is also more intense.

I remember that Zhang Xuefeng asked, "Is there an industry that is suitable for women?"* His answer was: "There isn't." His view is that women aren't good at professions that men are good at; they won't be suitable for these

* Zhang is an influential education entrepreneur and influencer.

positions. In jobs that are suitable for women, people will also think men are more competent.

One of my classmates from undergrad said that there was a person at her internship who always wanted to get close and touch her. He even called her in the middle of the night to ask where she lived. But she quickly put a stop to it, so nothing bad happened. Then last year a classmate of mine from grad school said the journalist who was her supervisor was pursuing her. She asked her academic advisor for help, and they let her leave the position quickly, so the situation ended.

If these things happened to me, I'd share it with friends, and then with classmates who study law. Then I'd talk to teachers who have more experience, since we have a good relationship with our advisors. If I'm harassed at work in the future I can talk to my teachers and they'll give some advice.

I Want to Have My Own Life and Be Economically Independent ASAP

When I first came here for the internship, I was by myself. After leaving work I'd go back to my rental alone, and would be by myself on the weekends too. It was hard to connect with coworkers to go out. I want to be in the same city as friends, but it's difficult because everyone makes different choices and the factors that go into their job selection are different, so this is just hopeful longing.

My family isn't in Q City, they are in D City [a prefecture in the same province] and of course they hope I stay in this province. But I think they haven't realized that I might have other possibilities—they reflexively think that it's better to be close to home. I just take their views as a point of reference, nothing more. Some neighboring provinces are still pretty close, and Q City is pretty far from D City. I can't just stay at home, I've always wanted to go out, and I'm fine with going far. Either way I'm leaving home. My hometown is a county within D City. They think that I've gotten so much education that I shouldn't go back to that small town, but they also don't want me to be too far away.

I'm not expecting my family to provide any more support; now that I'm over here in Q City there isn't anything they can do. So when it comes to my future job, I'm planning on depending on myself. My family is bent on me taking the civil service exam but they don't understand where I'm at these days. I don't have any time to study, and there's still pressure from my studies. So they just have their own opinions; they aren't giving me advice based on my actual situation. At the same time, they also want me to hurry up and get married or whatever.

I've been trying to instill in them the idea that I won't get married. They are of course traditional, and they hope that after I graduate and find work I'll get married and have kids. But I'm always telling them I'm thinking about not getting married. It's not even that I definitely won't get married, it's just that I'm trying to communicate to them that a life doesn't necessarily have to follow the prescribed order of marriage and kids, there are other options. You don't need to give weird looks to people who don't get married or have kids. I've found that they're gradually accepting this kind of idea; they've also seen on the internet that lots of young people aren't having kids. I want them to understand this issue.

When the government recruits civil servants, a lot of the positions target recent graduates. But this is mostly irrelevant for me.

I feel like the school mostly just wants to produce graduates and let us know about informational sessions. The college has also organized events on employment. Last year they invited two people from within the system to share their experiences, one from a state-owned enterprise [SOE] and one civil servant. It feels like everything revolves around the state system. But I feel like I have to do more to look for relevant recruitment information. The school isn't giving any more guidance.

I'll keep an eye out for SOE jobs. I feel like getting into the big companies is really hard, the competition is intense.

I think that I'll certainly be able to find a job. But this job might only be so-so. My college roommate graduated in the first half of this year and didn't find a job until just this month. She's been sending off her résumé nonstop. She got a master's degree from a non-elite school. She tried to get into so many companies, maybe her résumé wasn't up to speed, she was just always sending it out. She said that if your résumé isn't up to speed it's really hard to get a job. She didn't start her position until last week, and she was super anxious while waiting so long.

I want to find a job as soon as I graduate because I want to be economically independent and have my own life. I've spent so many years living as a student, a kind of collective life in the dormitories, and really want my own personal life. Plus, my parents wouldn't be able to accept it if I graduated but didn't have work. I'm definitely going to work right away.

I want to pursue long-term development. I have a classmate who was working in a company for two weeks and then discovered that the job didn't suit their professional development plans. So they quit and went to look for another job. If I'm in this kind of situation I would probably quit as long as I didn't have to pay too high a price for it; I wouldn't want to delay. If I had carefully thought it over before taking a job but then found a big gap between the reality and my expectations, or if it seemed like it wasn't helping my future, I think I'd still quit and find a job that suited my long-term development. But maybe I wouldn't be too annoyed doing this job, maybe every job is a kind of experience. I'm not particularly committed to getting into the system because I think life is a set of experiences. The kind of job I have, the kind of life I live, it's just these few years. After those years are over, then that's that. So, I'm just going to really experience life.

I'm looking forward to working in the future because I've wanted to hurry up and live my own life for too long. Now I'm rushing to find work and I think that after I land something my life will be enriched. I hope that after work I'll have time and enough money to pursue my interests and hobbies.

I'm a classic product of small town, test-focused education. My parents have only been concerned with my studies. I hope to be able to experience different kinds of things, but I'm embarrassed to tell my family I want to go do this or do that. I hope that after I'm working, I can do things like traveling or signing up for an exercise class.

Before, when I was doing my internship, I'd go out to eat or hang out with friends after work. Now I'm more worried about finding work because with the start of the semester and fall recruitment, our graduating group is receiving recruitment info, and we see this stuff every day. I also want to join an SOE, so I have to watch videos about the civil service exam. And now that school is in session my advisor is asking for my thesis. So now when I get off work, I feel very clearly that there isn't enough time, I'm quite busy. It's even harder to calm myself, it's not like my classmates who are doing test prep, they're just in the library fully devoted to studying for the exam. After work I don't have the thought or time to do test prep, maybe I'll just half-heartedly watch a video about the civil service exam. The things on the written test aren't that hard, I'll just try to learn a bit and that's it.

I really want a job and to know what's coming next, so I went to see a fortune teller. I did it back in February during Lunar New Year, and the fortune teller said that I wouldn't find work this year. Even though he said this I still need to do my best with the job search. I won't give up if I don't find anything during the fall recruitment. There's also spring recruitment, so I need to keep trying. Also, I know why he said I wouldn't find a job; he said I have too many different ideas and that I'm allowing my imagination to run wild.

I think I'll definitely find a job, but it will be a difficult journey. I need to keep searching, keep interviewing, and I might encounter frustrations and setbacks. I'm already emotionally prepared for this.

I plan to buy a home. I want my own house. I think my parents won't support me; they don't understand why they should help a woman buy her own house. But it's very hard to buy a house with the salary we can get with this major. Whatever, I can also just keep renting.

4

Why Is Finding Regular Work So Difficult?

I'm still looking for work. Here in Shandong it's basically impossible to get a regular job without connections. If you're looking for an eight-to-five job, basically you're not going to find it. Most jobs you'll earn around 2,000 to 3,000 yuan, and don't even think about social insurance.

My major was smart auto technology. Finding work is really hard. Our school only teaches us a bunch of random garbage, and we don't get any hands-on experience, they just send us out into the world. And these companies will only let you be an intern without the opportunity to convert to full-time employment. I already graduated a year ago and haven't found anything; I'm still trying to get people to help me out.

Student Zhang from Shandong,
2023 graduate, still unemployed

Passion Is Not Required for This Job

You need to complete an internship to graduate. A huge majority of the internship opportunities that the school provides are in an electronics factory. In the factory, those who have gone to school and those who haven't are all the same. In the second half of last year, my school's recruitment office sent me to an auto-parts manufacturer where I earned around 2,000 to 3,000 yuan a month.

This car company has been sourcing interns from the school for many years. It's an auto-parts supplier, mostly producing rearview mirrors, radar, and millimeter-wave radar.* When I was first reading about the company, it seemed like a reasonable place. Our school's upperclassmen recruited us and it was almost infectious, so I was duped into joining. The upperclassmen talked about when you could transition to a permanent position, the wages, and the content of the work, but when I actually joined the company, it wasn't exactly as they'd described.

Even though the company's high-end R&D is related to my major, interns don't get to use any of our skills at work, so being there doesn't do anything at all to improve our abilities. Sometimes I'd inspect some equipment, looking at various auto parts. I tested windshield wipers more than anything.

Even though the auto industry is booming, there are too many people trying to get a piece. Some foreign companies have really good wages and benefits, but private Chinese companies like ours are terrible. One of my classmates used their connections to get into a foreign firm and their base wage is 6,000 a month. Our base wage was 2,000 and we only got workplace injury insurance, none of the other

---

* This may refer to camera technology rather than just a physical mirror. But the phrase used is 后视镜, which literally means rearview mirror.

social insurance.* I was in the R&D department. If we performed well as a unit, they'd give us a bonus, but it didn't have much to do with individual effort. Regular employees got a wage of around 10,000 yuan, managers got roughly 30,000 to 40,000. The company hasn't been doing well these past few years, in the past regular employees could get a salary as high as 20,000 yuan.

My job didn't require any mental labor at all. Mostly I'd just make copies and print stuff or would go to the train station or airport to greet some leader. I did meaningless things every day and I gradually realized that you don't need any passion for this work. You can just muddle through and it's fine.

Pay for interns was completely dependent on the manager's mood. In the first month I got 4,000 because I was energetic. But my passion was gradually extinguished, and then they only gave me 2,000. My internship was in Jinan where rent alone costs 1,000, and the cafeteria has terrible food.† My monthly expenses were 2,000 to 3,000 yuan so there's no way I could save any money. Sometimes I had to ask my family for money. Food also isn't cheap. Our company was in a pretty remote location, and there aren't any small restaurants; getting takeout was about 20 yuan. I worked every day from eight until five, and sometimes the bosses grabbed our free time to hold a meeting. Some of the old

* The speaker refers to the "five insurances and one fund" which in addition to workplace injury insurance, includes coverage for pensions, parental leave, unemployment, and medical. The "one fund" is the housing provident fund.

† Jinan is the capital of Shandong province.

workers were pretty tough and ignored the manager; as soon as a meeting started, they'd just leave. One of these old workers used to be at the same rank as one of the managers here in Jinan. It was just that the manager had good luck, they had the right skills, and so they moved on up. This worker couldn't care less what the manager thinks.

I'm so disillusioned with the company. There was a female student who started there after me, who got into the company through personal connections and was immediately made a regular employee. I'm just extremely disillusioned. I came in July and she came in September. It wasn't until I had been working there for four or five months that I learned the company doesn't have any plans to expand recruitment, so I had no chance of becoming a regular employee. So I just left. There were three people in my internship group, now only one is left and they haven't been given a regular position. This company won't have more than fifty employees, because they want to stay small-scale.

I also became really disillusioned with my colleagues. HR was so obnoxious. If the company was out of printing paper or dry-erase pens, they'd ask you, "Why did you use them up so quickly? It's so wasteful." Sometimes we'd leave the office for meetings or to greet visiting leaders, and we needed to report our parking fees, and the garages need to issue a formal invoice. Lots of places can't give you anything other than a receipt, so you just have to pay for it yourself. The company was very stingy about turning on the heat in the winter; we couldn't use it until it hits a certain temperature. And we couldn't turn it on before 9 a.m. The climate control in our office was broken, and even though we asked to have it fixed, nobody came. I think that the HR rep was selling the workers out. He thinks he's part of ownership but actually they don't have any financial relationship at all. Why is he making life so difficult for everyone? I never understood why he was so hard on us—he even wanted to ration toilet paper. Some girls are kind of germaphobes, they cover the toilet seat with toilet paper before using it. The HR rep criticized them for this in a meeting.

Everyone in the company was indifferent to their colleagues and there is no cooperation; it's such a cold environment.

"Regular Employment" Is So Difficult

Those of us who majored in smart auto technology have to do sales if we want regular employment. I have no plans to go into sales. Auto sales is not a long-term profession, it requires youthful energy. I also think that the model of auto sales is outdated. Tesla has already introduced a new sales model, and this kind of job is going to be eliminated. In the last few years, a lot of people have been relocated because of redevelopment demolitions, and the economy has been growing. So a lot of people bought cars and the market is already saturated. Not many people are buying new cars anymore. I have classmates who have gone into sales and they're just barely getting by, living and eating at their parents' and earning the base wage of 800 yuan.

I also haven't given much thought to working in an electronics factory, it would just grind me down. Our teachers lied to us about working in these factories; they said we could work as technicians and earn 8,000 yuan. A classmate went to work in one. When they came back they straight up said they'd been duped, the salary wasn't 8,000 yuan, and they weren't working as a technician. The reality was they were working on the assembly line.

I'm very frustrated looking for work, I've already tried lots of different things. My hometown is a fourth-tier city, and there are no decent jobs. Around here, recruitment software [Boss, 58.com] is just a platform for fraud. The postings only become a bit more normal after you change your search region to a first- or second-tier city. Around here you can't find regular work if you don't have connections. It's nearly impossible to find the kinds of jobs that have standard working hours and social insurance benefits.

I've had two interviews in other cities. I went to Xiangshan County in Ningbo to interview at a company that does testing of car shock absorbers and drive-by-wire chassis. But they wanted someone with a more advanced degree. The other time I interviewed was with an internet company in a university entrepreneurship park in Hangzhou. The employees were pretty young, the management seemed innovative, and the overall vibe pretty good. I failed this time because they wanted someone with different training. It's a small company that works on directing internet traffic. They had so many interviewees, and I was rejected. I didn't get a direct explanation for why I failed either of these interviews, and I didn't want to ask.

I apply for any kind of job that I can do: IT, international e-commerce, foreign trade. I'd like to do foreign trade, but finding a reliable company is not easy.

The Employment Environment Is Bad, So I Want to Go Abroad

My family's annual income is around 300,000; it's relatively good. But this is not the life I imagined. My dad works in construction as a labor contractor, and his income is really unstable; sometimes he's earning a lot, other times he'll go a full year without earning anything. I never want to do this kind of work. I've been unemployed for a year, but my family isn't worried. They want me to join the military to put off looking for work for a few years. If not, then they want me to get married. I'm not interested in either of these. My goal for the next few years is to go abroad, but they think that you shouldn't leave unless you're starving. What if you go abroad and something happens? They would be worried.

The employment environment in China is really bad. Lots of companies don't think of labor law as real law. So many people I know are extremely ignorant and things that I think are normal seem really weird to them. When I left my last job, they still hadn't paid me, but they sent me my paycheck later on. My mom was like, "Wow, what a good company, they paid you even after you left!"

My classmates are also having a rough time looking for work. So many people are trying to get into grad school; half of my classmates are going to take the exam. I think applying to grad school is just avoiding reality, and they know this. Then some other people are leaning on personal connections to get work. Our school is just a pathetic second-rate university. If you can find a decent job, you've done well. There are forty people in our class and about ten haven't found work. I'm regularly in touch with two others who haven't found anything.

If your family has some money, then finding work isn't so urgent. My family has savings of 2 to 3 million, so my family's only goal is for me to find a wife; they don't mind if I just hang out every day. Some parents think that their kids are still young, it's OK for them to mess around for another couple of years. A lot of these families have their own small businesses, and they think the kid can take it over. I don't want to do this.

I want to go abroad and get residency and go back to school for a few years. I don't want to study cars anymore; I've already been led astray. In auto programming you need to study so much and it's so hard, but I've already mostly forgotten everything. You need practice to be able to do assembly and design and those kinds of things. I've become interested in psychology. I think that communicating with other people is relaxing. I tend to be quite reflective, and I've been reading some really interesting books on psychology. It's also a kind of self-soothing; if I didn't have these books I wouldn't know what to do with myself. I really like chatting with friends about what they've been up to, or about the state of the world. All my friends and I like to commiserate by complaining, by blaming everyone but ourselves.

Young People Have Some Breathing Room; There's No Need for Them to Rush into Work

Our parents' generation suffered so much, and they don't want us to be miserable, so they won't criticize you if you can't find work. I think this is why unemployment is so high. These days young people have some breathing room. If we didn't have a buffer and the unemployment rate was this high, of course we'd revolt.

Some friends from my hometown have opened pet stores, gaming venues, barbecue restaurants, or lottery-ticket shops. You don't really make or lose money with the lottery tickets. You can't drive for the on-demand platforms anymore, there are too many and the market for drivers is already saturated. I've thought about opening a teahouse. The goal of working should be to realize your personal values. Your beliefs will evolve as you mature, so even if I'm doing auto and smart technology or whatever right now, eventually I might open a teahouse.

The world has been giving me all these frustrations; it's really a lot to deal with. Our sources of information are a mess now. Chinese media doesn't have any journalistic energy, they are always presenting things out of context. For example, the panda, Yaya.* I've never bought the story that she was mistreated; how could a normal person believe that a country would mistreat an animal? It's the same with

* Yaya is a panda who was based at a zoo in Memphis until 2023. Amid intensifying US-China hostility, some suggested that Yaya's poor appearance—she suffered from a skin condition—was due to her maltreatment.

the floods, it's so annoying.* I rarely watch the news, and I only see foreign media when my friends repost it, since I don't know how to get it (you need to download some software). But I know what's good.

Right now, I'm lying flat. I don't think producing offspring is the most important thing in life; it's about creating some kind of value. Let's say you have a kid: Can you give them a decent life? Can you give them more choices? You shouldn't be bringing life into this world just for them to suffer, it should be to enjoy life. Nobody wants kids these days; maybe things will be better in ten years. I don't know what's going to happen next, I'm very confused about the future.

* Numerous places in China suffered flooding in 2023, including Beijing and the surrounding region.

5

Low Wages and Low Pressure: The Semi-Lying-Flat Work of a Private School Teacher

This interviewee is a young woman who graduated in 2022 with a master's degree from a university in Changsha. Now she's teaching at a private university in Changsha with a monthly salary of 4,000 to 5,000 yuan. She's mostly satisfied with her work and doesn't have too many expenses. But she is quite disturbed by the employment landscape and labor rights issues.

Fulan from Hunan, 2022 graduate,
teacher in a private school

I Ended Up Choosing a Job with Lower Wages Than I Had Expected

I originally expected to get a job that paid 5,000 to 6,000 yuan per month. But when I was looking for work, things got held up by the company I was interning for. So I couldn't start the job search until the end of April, nearly till May. This meant I missed out on the spring and fall recruitment drives, and it was extremely close to my graduation. I also had to finish my thesis right then, so I only got two interviews.

I found an internship at a state-owned publishing house during the fall recruitment before graduation. I did a one-week internship there, and a manager told me that most interns can stay on in a regular position. He said the ratio was really high, that out of twenty or thirty people, only one or two wouldn't stay. I thought that my chances of getting a job were quite good, so I didn't put much effort into applying elsewhere. But it turned out that they dissolved the department I was interning in and they didn't retain more than a few people. I kept asking the HR department if I would be kept on, but they never responded. It wasn't until March that they told me I wouldn't be able to stay. This is why I didn't start looking for work until April or May of this year. I argued with HR, telling them that they need to inform people more quickly, but the company held things up for so long, and I missed a lot of opportunities to apply for jobs.

After I had an interview with this private university, they told me that the job was mine. I asked them about the salary during the interview, and it was less than I had expected, but it wasn't off by too much. I was also considering my academic qualifications and the typical salaries in this area. I graduated with a master's degree from a top-tier local university. This is a new first-tier city, so living expenses including rent are more like a second-tier city. So rent and the cost of living aren't too bad. Given all these factors, and because I wanted to get things sorted out ASAP, I thought that working in a school would be relatively solid. As a teacher in a university, you don't have that much stress at work and you get winter and summer breaks. And I like teaching and pedagogy. So I decided to yield on the lower-than-expected salary. I also think that work stress and salary are directly proportional, including in my current job. So I'm pretty satisfied at the moment.

An Ideal Job Allows You to Realize Your Values

At a minimum, having a job should ensure your basic needs; you need social insurance and these kinds of basic protections. And second, you should be able to recognize the value of the work. There are some lines of work that I just can't see the value of, like finance. Of course, it's not that they're totally useless, but as far as I'm concerned doing finance isn't as valuable as being a health care worker. It depends on your perspective.

Work intensity is not the only thing that matters; not all ideal jobs are relaxed. It isn't too realistic to expect a job that is never intense, but at a minimum it wouldn't extinguish your humanity. There are some specific jobs, like public interest work, that can be more intense. But you won't feel exploited in these jobs, despite the work's intensity. Of course, it's a problem that wages in these jobs are so low. Some people even say things like, "You're doing public interest work, why do you also want to make a living?" This is really upsetting. People look at these workers as subhuman; they're just ignoring their human value.

As far as I'm concerned, work has to allow you to realize your values, otherwise it would be very hard to do it long term. I think being a teacher is meaningful work because you can have a positive influence on other people. My students are relatively old, and their basic values are mostly formed, but I can still provide a little bit of a different perspective, which I think is a plus. It gives me a real sense of accomplishment. At least it's a job that you won't hate yourself for; that could really make someone go insane.

The Government Puts the Responsibility on Our Shoulders

The labor market was already not great when I had just started university. When I was a freshman, the government began promoting the "mass entrepreneurship and innovation" initiative. They wanted to encourage students to be entrepreneurial while still in school, to stimulate the economy. The policy has been like this right up till now. I think the way the government wants to deal with unemployment is to put the responsibility on our shoulders. Recently there was a viral article imploring students to "take off Kong Yiji's robe," meaning that we shouldn't be so choosy about jobs.* When I read this article, I was enraged. According to the article, us undergrad and graduate students have too much confidence in our degrees, we're aloof and self-important, so we refuse to do those low-wage jobs.

But it's not like this; it's not that young people are unwilling to take these jobs. Just taking the people that I know as an example, their salaries are a bit higher, maybe 2,000

* Kong Yiji is a well-known character in a short story by Lu Xun. In the story, Kong refuses to take off his scholar's robe even though he has failed to pass the civil service exam. In the contemporary iteration, state media have implored university-educated youth to accept whatever job they can find, regardless of whether it fulfills their aspirations.

yuan more than mine. But they have to work ten or more hours every day. Has the government thought about the kinds of jobs out there for young people, and the fact that some people are trying to balance work and life? They are asking young people to devote themselves, but the returns for this devotion are really limited. Young people are under a lot of pressure, including pressure to support their elders. Pensions are inadequate; everyone is gradually pushing back the retirement age. There are so many of these kinds of problems. But the government wants to push these problems onto individuals rather than trying to do something.

The labor market in Changsha is so terrible, and everybody says that this city is outside the bounds of the Labor Law.* In Changsha, there are extremely few jobs that have two days off a week; either you get one day off, or they have big/small weeks.† I'm not exactly sure if other cities are like this. But I think that the government and supervisory departments have a very big responsibility to regulate the labor market and to implement every single provision in the Labor Law. This includes regulating working hours and social insurance; these are all basic things. I read this article that talked about how everyone is very concerned with social insurance when they're looking for work, but a lot of people don't understand how social insurance funding works or how these welfare programs protect us. Legal dissemination hasn't been very good; when people have

* This is not literal; it is meant to suggest that labor laws are not rigorously enforced.

† This means workers alternate between five- and six-day workweeks.

their rights violated, they aren't sure how to address it or what rights they even have. The government can improve labor law education.

When the National Bureau of Statistics stopped releasing the unemployment rate, they were just burying their heads in the sand.* I think they believed the numbers were too embarrassing; there's no way it was because there were some changes in the methodology. It's just so ridiculous. You can use a new methodology and continue releasing the data. But I think that releasing the unemployment rate would cause people to lose faith in the labor market; maybe this is what the officials were considering. But you can't stop releasing the data just because you don't want people to lose faith. You can't have blind faith while sweating away trying to find work, people need to have some idea about labor market conditions. I really hated what they did.

Schools and Advisors Fabricate Data and Harass Students in Order to Boost Their Employment Numbers

I'm not sure what the situation is like in grad schools, but when I was an undergrad, the school was fabricating employment numbers. They obviously know that some students don't have a job, or that they're going to apply to grad school. But they will force these students to find any old workplace or a family member's company to sign an

* In 2023 the government suddenly stopped releasing data on youth unemployment, see: Mariko Oki and Nick Marsh, "China Suspends Youth Unemployment Data After Record High," bbcnews.com.

employment contract, and this is how they improve the school's employment rate. I had a roommate who couldn't find a job; one month before graduation, their advisor started calling them every day. The class director would also come chat with them all the time.

When I had my first interview, the interviewer asked me to do a three-minute self-introduction. I had no experience with this kind of formal interview, and the experience I had with my earlier internship was completely unrelated. So I completely froze up. I think I said the same thing over and over again like four or five times. Our school could have given us some basic help prepping for interviews. My college had a public social media account specifically for giving us job recruitment info. But it was totally focused on things just related to the major; those were the only things they would post. Speaking as someone who doesn't really want to do work related to this major, if this was the only channel, my sources of information would be very limited. I had to go looking for things on my own, and I got a lot of info about recruitment from other schools' websites. I think that our school could have more diverse recruitment info.

Schools could do more to support their students' job searches. To start with, while we're still in school they could develop our professional interests by giving us more internship opportunities. This could happen as soon as we start our degree, instead of in our final year before graduation. It doesn't even have to be a long-term thing. I did a weeklong internship, and these kinds of short-term experiences give us the opportunity to learn what various kinds of jobs are really like. This would be better than sending people into full-time employment as a blank slate. Also, I think schools could give their students more info on employment. Even if they don't have any specific info, they could tell us about various sources of information. I think this would be a great approach. Finally, when it comes time to sign contracts, schools could give their students some more protection. They could learn about the kinds of conditions existing employees have.

Involution Is a Vicious Cycle, and Lying Flat Is Passive Resistance

I really hate involution, I think it's such a vicious cycle. It's based on the idea that we should see other people as enemies. I'm not exactly sure what this kind of company culture is like, but I think that when you're in this sort of environment you see everyone as your competition for getting a promotion or retaining your job. So I really don't like involution, but maybe it's also impossible for people to avoid this kind of situation. Maybe companies are intentionally creating these kinds of systems. They rank everyone's working hours, then rank their Key Performance Indicators, and this creates a competitive environment for everyone. It seems like these environmental factors are quite important.

Lying flat seems like passive resistance; maybe it's just a kind of exhaustion. I know some people who are really lying flat, their living expenses are super low and their income is also super low. They keep their desires and consumption at a basic subsistence level. But I don't think this kind of life is necessarily easier. I'm not completely lying flat, but I'm also not all in on involution. People often say that they're envious of my job, but I feel like if I offered my low-wage job to them they actually wouldn't want it.

I don't have to provide for anyone, I'm not married, I don't own a car or house, and don't have kids. But a lot of people do have these expenses and for them it's so hard to take a job that has low wages or is unstable. These kinds of family pressures really are some of the most important factors. Educational background also has a big impact on employment. When I was looking for work, I submitted my résumé to lots of schools. Now they aren't only concerned with your graduate degree, they also want to look at your undergrad education. In addition to graduate degrees, they'll use undergrad degrees to evaluate people and filter some of them out. If you want to work in an SOE, or as a civil servant or public employee, your degree is a *super* basic requirement. But if you're an entrepreneur or doing flexible employment, of course it's not as important.

I used to think that I didn't like education as a profession. But then I discovered I was interested in it, and that I wanted to keep doing this kind of work even if it wasn't in this specific job. But I'm not very optimistic about the salary. As for the future, I think that if there aren't huge changes in government policy and social conditions then the job market won't get any better. It's just going to get worse, and everyone's mental health will also get worse.

6

Giving Up a University Diploma and Finding Another Path

I was a computer science major at a medical college. I wasn't originally interested in this major, but my older brother and high school teacher suggested it. I also thought it wasn't bad to follow the trend, so I ended up choosing this major. My dad didn't understand what a CS major would do after graduation. He's a carpenter and thought that I should learn a trade, but my mom wanted me to get an education so I could be a little more relaxed in the future. They do interior renovation. Most tile workers and carpenters are pretty old; most are older than forty or fifty. There's not too many young people. These trades will probably not have enough people in the future because the cost of labor has gone up. I'm interested in going to study tile work and carpentry, these kinds of skilled trades. Some adults think young people can just earn money using their cell phones instead of doing physical labor. But I still haven't completely made up my mind about switching to carpentry and tile work.

Student from Shandong, graduated
in 2022, software programmer

I Don't Want to Fight the Test-Based System, Just to Find a Different Path

Schools in Anhui aren't great. When I was in high school, I didn't even understand the concept of a "major." Now some universities are changing; in your first year you just take intro courses before choosing a major.* I think this is an improvement. According to Zhang Xuefeng, there aren't many good majors to choose from when taking the university entrance exam. Especially in my high school, students know that if they study, they can test into university, but they don't actually know anything about universities. There doesn't necessarily need to be a connection between your major and your personal interests. I think it's great if you can work while in high school. Instead of going to cram schools during winter and summer breaks, you can get a job and meet some people. This way you can chat with folks to learn about and experience society.

I wasn't at all interested in CS in my first few years in university. I was pretty confused. From freshman to junior year, I barely went to class. I hadn't found any motivation or meaning in my studies, so I hadn't completed the requirements for my major and couldn't get my diploma. I want to broaden my path and give myself more choices. I don't even want to fight the test-based system; I just want to find a different path.

---

* In China, students have typically had to choose their major before enrolling in university.

I've started following an organization in Guangzhou called Practical School that I saw someone repost on social media.* They do professional training instead of regular degree-granting education. A lot of rural kids can't get into high school, their scores are only good enough to go to technical schools. A lot of people can't adapt and are unhappy. The Practical School allows people in this kind of situation to continue to develop. If they are physically and emotionally healthy, this is already pretty incredible. I'm wondering if I might be able to get a job there as a teacher in four or five years.

When I was in my senior year of university, I connected with a professor online. He was looking for someone who didn't have experience with programming to help him complete a textbook aimed at students with no foundation in CS. I fitted the description, so I applied to join the experimental course.† I was so happy in this course, and I gradually became interested in CS.

My Search for a Career: Coder, Kindergarten Programming Teacher, Massage Therapist

In my senior year of university, I joined an internet training course organized by a vocational college. This course was sponsored by a company, so we didn't have to pay tuition. We just had to pay for room and board; the other expenses

---

* 实务学堂

† Presumably he fitted the description because he hadn't taken his studies seriously.

were covered by the company and the local government. The school recommended internships for us and I easily transitioned to working at a company. I didn't have to do overtime in my department, the work schedule was eight hours a day, five days a week. I decided to quit after only two or three months, but I heard that the other students who had started at the same time as I did stuck around.

I quit because I was extremely uncomfortable with the work environment. I had some conflicts with the boss and was even forced into a face-to-face argument with him. I remember that the other interns would quietly cheer me on for being so brave. But also, I discovered that this job didn't require me to use any of my programming skills. It was more like a filing and document-management job, and I was eager to gain knowledge and learn new skills. I was worried that if I stuck with this kind of job, it would limit my opportunities for growth in the future.

As a CS major it was pretty easy for me to find internship opportunities. But finding a job that I actually liked was hard. Of course the salary is an important factor to consider, but the work also has to challenge you and provide a sense of satisfaction. If the work seems like a middle school student could do it, then it isn't challenging. I'm not that interested in or motivated by work anymore; it's been gradually replaced by other things.

From April to June, I had my second internship. This was at a startup company, and the work environment wasn't bad. My internship wages were 3,500 yuan per month, and it would go up to 5000 for regular employees. They also provided housing. But then there were some scheduling conflicts when I had to go back to school, so I ended up leaving the company.

I had a friend who had always wanted to go to Yantai;* he had heard that it was a good spot. I wasn't thinking about going at first, but I started to get interested after listening to him, so I decided to go have a look for myself. I started submitting job applications right in the middle of graduation season, so the competition was extremely intense. I eventually found a company that was willing to hire me, so I made up my mind and went. Looking back on it, that decision was a little scary. To be honest, when I got to Yantai I felt like I had been led to a strange kind of place—I was hired to teach programming in a kindergarten for a tutoring company. These were the two most difficult months I had experienced since high school, even more difficult than the lead-up to the university entrance exam. I had long working hours, the wages were low, and the work intensity was high.

I really disagree with this company's approach to education. I feel like they are being kind of dishonest in how they do things. Their approach is deceptive, and this deception is not limited to this particular organization; the entire system is deceptive. I feel like the whole system is like a scam syndicate, it's just awful. Up at the top they plan some programming competitions, then we have to convince parents that their kids won't succeed in life unless they participate. This makes parents feel anxious. It's just an industrial approach to defrauding people.

---

* A medium-sized city on the coast of Shandong Province.

On top of that, the wages at that company were extremely low. We only got 5 yuan for each student in an hour-long class, and this is not enough for me. The teacher that earned the most money in that company would only make 5,000-plus per month. And he already had a full workload, but that was all he earned. I was so busy because there was another teacher who was sick, and I helped cover some of his classes. After each class I was exhausted. How many students did we have in each class? Each class had eight, or sometimes up to nine. Since I got 5 yuan per student, with that head count I could only make 40 yuan per class. And you also needed to spend time helping them to review and teaching them how to express the things they'd learned so that the parents would feel like the kids actually learned something there. I think that my work was mostly emotional labor. It was exhausting and really made me suffer. Teachers really have it rough.

Interestingly, I began to tutor some kids on my own. This allowed me to choose my own teaching materials without being restricted to the company's content. This was more interesting for me. I remember getting programming exercises from some foreign grad students to give to my students. At the end of the summer I left that company and moved to a new city. Then I completely ran out of money and couldn't pay the bills. I ran out of options, so around the winter solstice I went to learn to do massage. The massage parlor I ended up at provided room and board, so at least I could survive. And it isn't difficult to be a massage therapist. As long as you're willing to learn, you can make do.

I remember that I did it for over two months. I trained quickly, I just did seven days and then I could start working. At first, I had a master looking after me to teach me some things, but then he quit. Over the next two or three weeks various people would teach me, but everyone was teaching me different methods; it was a bit chaotic. But it was kind of exciting, like I was being mentored by a series of martial arts masters. Sometimes I would feel frustrated because some of their teaching methods and skills were in conflict. Once, I was being impatient and scraped my hand while practicing back massage.

I finally saw the light after an older worker reminded me that I can't expect instant success. After that, management thought that I'd become lazy and that I wasn't working very hard to learn new skills. The reality was that I wanted to master a new technique (like back massage), and I became kind of obsessive. At first, my hands were very rigid and my fingers weren't flexible enough; I wasn't up to speed, especially on back massages. But I gradually improved my technique. I had only mastered a few techniques when I left that place, including foot, back, and head massage and a few spa techniques.* People prefer female to male masseuses. And you don't really earn money just doing massage, it's mostly a way to learn various sales techniques.†

---

* "Spa" is written in English, but there is no explanation of what these techniques include.

† This is not elaborated, but perhaps the implication is that they try to sell additional products to the customers.

I remember perfectly that my first month's wages were 550 yuan. I'd worked for ten-plus days and each day I only got one customer because we were still being impacted by the pandemic. I'd get a cut of just 40 yuan for each customer. So each day I only earned 40 yuan, and my monthly wage wasn't much. And I didn't start working until the middle of the month, so I earned even less. Things improved a little bit later, but not by much. The market started to gradually recover at the end of last year, and I went to some shop in Yantai to help out. After that I went back to the previous place, but their business was still bad.

There's No Overtime Pay Without a Fight

At the end of the year, I came back to Yantai to look for a new job. I searched for a month before finding something, the same job that I have now. The awkward thing was that during interviews with some internet companies I realized that I don't have any work experience. I didn't want to try to fake it, so I didn't ask for a high salary; I'd take anything related to IT work. But the result of this was that I didn't find anything at all. My boss at my current job might think that I have a bit of relevant experience, but they also really needed someone, so they decided to give me a shot. Things have gone smoothly. It's a software engineer position and the job isn't hard. The company is family owned and there aren't too many employees—many employees are the boss's relatives. But the boss doesn't have a great reputation. A lot of welders and machinists won't work at this company. Even if they offered higher wages they wouldn't come here, because in the past the company had problems with unpaid wages, and the boss hasn't kept his promises. So this company has been blacklisted.*

But I mostly trust my manager; he's a university professor and hasn't picked up the boss's bad habits. The work environment isn't so terrible, it's just that the company doesn't have clearly defined rules. It seems like everything depends on the boss's mood. We don't get any overtime pay without fighting for it; otherwise you tacitly accept to give it up. We also have to work on Saturdays even though there isn't that much to do.

There are fewer than twenty people in the company. It's a tech company focused on automated assembly lines. The company's survival depends on government support; the assembly line still has a lot of problems and hasn't met market requirements. Private companies can't afford our automated assembly lines, so the government is in the background picking up the tab [actually it's SOE-subsidiary companies]. The automated production should be able to handle 10,000 units but the truth is it can only manage to produce 1,000 and the remaining 9,000 are done manually by people. It's basically spending money just for show, and it's dependent on local government support. Maybe because it's a traditional industry, doing software work is relatively relaxed; it's not as exhausting as in those IT companies. They decided to hire me, even though I've never worked in an IT company, so I still don't really know what they are

---

* This is not an official blacklist. He is merely referring to the way workers shun employment there because of its reputation.

like. There is the problem of unpaid wages, and before I came the company was really in the red. In two years, they only paid wages four times.

Staying on Your Toes to Find a Job

Schools are extremely concerned with their students' employment, even if you're applying to grad school. They are very anxious to have students give them info about internships or employment, so that they can meet the quotas assigned to them by the higher-ups. Because of this, a lot of students randomly pick the name of a company so they can get the schools off their backs. Our advisors teach us how to write a résumé and give us some introduction to how recruitment works. But looking back on it now, I don't think this info was much help.

Why is it like this? Maybe it's because this information is too general and not specific enough. I relied more on doing my own searching or asking alumni for advice; these things have been more useful. The reality is that a successful job search might need to be more spontaneous. You can't just rely on others' recommendations.

My mom has supported my choices; I guess I've brainwashed her and she thinks it's OK that I don't have a diploma [laughs]. I changed work a lot last year, and each time I moved I needed to rent a place. My mom has covered the rent for me. I was quite volatile then, but now that I've settled down a bit I'm paying her back. My parents don't have any expectations of me. My mom panicked when she first heard from my teachers that I wouldn't graduate. But later she saw that it wouldn't have too big an impact on my job search. I told her that I had already learned the most important things and I discussed my education with her. Eventually she saw that things were just going to be like this, but occasionally she'll still urge me to go back and finish my degree. When I completely gave up on it, she also decided to lie flat.

Those Who Have Jobs Didn't Do Well in School

I think that the high youth unemployment is because of the government. A lot of companies went under because of the pandemic policies; it was very difficult for them to survive. A lot of materials need to be brought in and processed before they can be sold again, so there were problems as soon as logistics broke down. If companies didn't have enough reserves they would be drained. Companies can manage certain kinds of losses and not others, and if it's the latter they have to close down. I know a lot of people from the earlier generation who can't find work, I'm not sure why. The economy has become extremely bad, and I think it's the government's fault and responsibility.

I feel like a lot of graduates won't want to look for work because the job market isn't good. Most are tending to take the grad school exam or civil service exam. There's clearly something wrong here. Among people I know, the ones that have jobs didn't do well in school, just like me.

7

Life or High Wages, You Can Choose Only One: Resolving Involution Requires More Resistance

I graduated from a second-tier science and engineering school in 2021. Finding work wasn't that hard because it's a STEM school. I went to a campus job fair and found a job at a publicly listed auto company in my hometown, D City [a first-tier city in the south]. But the work environment was oppressive. At the beginning of this year, I moved to K City [a first-tier city on the east coast] for a job. I'm doing nine to five right now, but I'm stressing a bit about the salary.

Xiao Mian from the south, 2021 graduate
of a science and engineering school, working
in a private company in a first-tier city

I Was Confused After Graduating, and Just Wanted to Find Something to Get By

I took the grad school entrance exam before graduation, but I failed. I was feeling confused and just wanted to find something to get by for a bit. I checked out some recruitment sites, but the information was uneven and hard to filter. My school is in the north, but my hometown is in the south, and I wanted to go back to the south for work. At the campus recruitment event I found something that seemed appropriate and like I was a good fit, so I applied. There aren't that many companies close to my hometown, and I don't really know much about what's happening there. Everything went pretty smoothly with the application.

At the time I felt like I would be able to find a job if I wanted to. The job fair was quite lively and there were lots of matches. Our school is industry-focused, so the kinds of companies that our majors connect with are SOEs, construction companies, the National Railway Administration, or boiler plants, and they can absorb all our graduates. These companies might not be that famous but they're doing very practical work.

The school's support has been very effective, but we haven't gotten much help from the government. They might organize a job fair in the city, but nobody I know has found work this way.

My family didn't give me any help either, but they also haven't tried to interfere in my decisions. I asked them if I should choose x or y, and they said whichever one was closer to home so that they could give me some support and I could go home on the weekends for a meal. Some people's families own a factory or something like that, so they can get a job there. I'm not sure if I know anyone who got a job this way. I just hope that my family doesn't force me to constantly go do things that I don't want to do. This is actually the biggest help they can give me. A lot of people don't find their way right after graduation, and based on what

I've heard, families can really help by letting them hang out for a year and giving them food and a place to stay. If you want to take the civil service exam you'll need to first enroll in courses, like interview courses, comprehensive courses, etc., which might cost tens of thousands of yuan. Some people are definitely being supported by their families.

My job doing procurement mostly requires communicating and negotiating, reminding our suppliers to finish our orders while cutting costs, and guaranteeing timely delivery so that business can proceed smoothly. Usually, I'm just sitting in the office from morning till night. In my opinion you can do this job if you've graduated high school, know how to talk to people, and can be a little flexible. We purchase some industrial products, and this can involve some product selection, which requires a little bit of specialization. But it's not that hard; if you put in a little effort you can take care of it. You can look at the education of people in our office: Some of the people in procurement with more experience graduated from technical college. But among the batch of college recruits, there are some with graduate degrees from 211 universities, and there are some wage gaps. In my opinion, procurement isn't highly skilled work, but you do need experience. There is a lot to learn, especially when it comes to setting up your network. This has to be accumulated over time.

Procurement is kind of a sensitive job and there are a lot of restrictions. You can't just go out for meals with whomever you like and you have to keep your hands clean. When one of our suppliers exposed corruption by someone from our department, they were fired.

Wages and benefits were pretty decent for those that were hired at the same time as me. Pretax wages were around 6,000. The company is a "key enterprise," so I also received a human capital subsidy from D City. This came out to an additional 1,200 per month for people with undergrad degrees, and if you got it for three years that would come out to be around 40,000. With a grad degree you would get a bit more. Our company also provides housing; it's like public housing with two people to a room. Postgrads can get a single room. This isn't bad in a place like D City.

My Previous Company Was a Trap: They Broke Their Recruitment Promises

I used to work at an alternative-energy auto company; it's been facing huge challenges in the last couple of years. It's been about one year since I left, and the company has undergone massive changes. Like they used to provide housing, but that's been canceled. Lots of departments have had layoffs or people have left on their own.

This company would bring in a lot of new graduates through campus recruitment each year. But it's pretty inhumane. This year they ended up rejecting about three hundred graduates who had already signed an agreement. At first the company asked if they'd be willing to change their position, like if their original position was as a technician they'd be asked to change to being a program manager. Of course people refused this because they basically all had engineering graduate degrees from 211 schools. If the original position had a pretty good salary and was a good skills match, and then suddenly graduates were asked to be program managers instead, of course that would be hard for them to accept. Later, the company straight up fired the whole group. The original agreement is tripartite [between the school, the company, and the graduates] and not a labor contract, so each person only got 2,000 yuan in compensation. I think it's totally unconscionable. A lot of graduate students are looking for work because they need to support their families, and there could be some people who already have a mortgage. By violating their agreement during the recruitment season, which is such a sensitive moment, the company only left the graduates with a very small window to still look for work. It's such a trap, but there's nothing they can do.

This was reported in the media and lots of people were posting it on Zhihu and Bilibili, so others could avoid the storm.* But to be honest, it didn't make that big a splash. This is a relatively small publicly-listed company, but in IT or some other industries this kind of thing is extremely common; some even bigger companies have stooped to this kind of trickery. These individualized attacks are pretty common, but maybe this is just about the company's reputation within the industry. They're still doing campus recruitment, they're still bringing in new graduates. But if graduates ask alumni, learn that the company is a complete disaster, and go somewhere else, there'd be nothing that the company could do.

* Zhihu is often compared to Quora and Bilibili is a video sharing site.

Sometimes I Feel Helpless; You Have to Choose Between Earning Money and Feeling Relaxed

I was totally exhausted at my last job. Industrial jobs start early in the morning: You have to be there by 8 a.m. and then there is overtime every day. As soon as you finish dinner you have to do overtime until eight at night. We got 12 yuan an hour for overtime. This isn't even as much as the hourly rate for workers in a supermarket. In the evening I'd get back to the dorms around nine, but even then I might still have to take calls. Once I took a day off and my phone was ringing nonstop all afternoon; it was like they couldn't survive without me. But what are they even calling about? It's always some procedural issue, reviewing the same things over and over. Some companies' workflows get all messed up once they get a little larger. One issue will constantly be reviewed by this manager, then by that manager, then you're getting pressure from some other direction, and it feels like being in a whirlpool. It's so exhausting and makes me feel like I need to take a break. If something goes wrong, then some of the managers will try to blame you. They want you to shoulder the blame because you're just a low-level procurement officer; they won't try to defend you. And after the meeting they won't come by and be like, "This has been tough on you, you're doing a good job," or anything like that.

We were doing big/small weeks. One week we'd get two days off and the next week one and a half days off. But each department was different. In the procurement department we did a half day on Saturdays for our little week, but the tech department might have to hold meetings and do a whole day on Saturday. The company encourages overtime, so sometimes we just held a meeting or whatever. Of the four weeks in a month there are two small weeks, so that equals an extra full day of work each month. Since the company is publicly listed and they want to pretty themselves up, they counted that one day off as paid sick leave, the kind that is optional. They even counted this as part of our benefits package [laughs]. But if you took paid sick leave then you didn't get your attendance bonus, which was only 50 yuan per month.

I worked at that company for one year, from right after I graduated until I left in summer 2022. I took a little break after that, and then after New Year my boyfriend and I moved to K City and gradually started to look for work. I looked for work online and I think it went pretty smoothly. I have a nine-to-five job now, and like before, I'm doing procurement for industrial materials. I'm working as a business agent for M, a foreign company. I used to do purchases from M in my previous job and now I'm in procurement at M's distributor, so it's like I've moved down a level. But it's less stressful than before and I sleep well every night. There are fewer procedures in a small company. This company only has forty or fifty people so there's less annoying stuff to deal with. M has a pretty central location in the production chain; a few key parts have to be imported, so it's easy to sell their products.

Now I get all the normal holidays. We never do overtime, by 5 p.m. everyone is ready to leave and basically everyone is gone right on the dot. In my free time I like to read books, do some exam prep, or just hang out a bit. Sometimes I'll cook a meal; I hardly had any time to cook before. I can do all kinds of things now when I'm not at work.

I think that work is just work, and I've already started to lie flat. For now, I just need to earn enough to support myself and just get by, and I'll see where I want to go next. Sometimes I feel helpless; you have to choose between earning money and feeling relaxed. My salary is pretty low right now and my company doesn't provide housing. In a new city like K, life is a bit stressful.

I'm not sure why, but I feel like whenever my family sees me relaxing, they get anxious. I don't know, maybe it's that they're used to being oppressed so they think young people can't work hard and that we'll suffer in the future. They've always been very demanding of me, they always want to push me to do better. They thought my last job must have been good; after all, it's publicly listed! The job allowed me to take on a lot of responsibilities, so they thought it was pretty good. They weren't at all worried that I was exhausted or in a bad place emotionally. They just thought that since I'm young, why should I have these problems? Now that I've moved to K City, they have some opinions about this because I came here with my boyfriend and now I'm apart from them. I quit my last job suddenly and didn't have a plan for what would come next. When I suddenly moved to K City maybe they thought that I don't have any plans and am lost in life. And my salary isn't that high anymore, so they're like, "How come we're still working so hard and you're just lying flat and rotting away every day?" They have some things they'd like to tell me.

We Need More People to Resist

To begin with, various market demands are already relatively saturated and conservative. Among my friends, those with liberal arts degrees have had an extremely hard time finding work, and the same goes for programmers. I have a friend who is a programmer and a graduate from a 985 university. They started looking for work at the same time as me in the beginning of the year, and they still haven't found anything. There are also lots of layoffs happening now, including at my old company. A lot of former technicians in our group chat are beaten down, saying things like, "Thanks for the memories, next time will be even better." Among those who came via campus recruitment at the same time as me, which was between two hundred and three hundred people, barely any are still at the company. A huge majority have left for various places to find work.

A lot of other people are highly educated but have relatively simple jobs. My undergrad degree is from a non-elite university, but the procurement work that I'm doing now only requires a high school degree and the ability to use a computer. So why do they need to hire someone with a university degree? Doesn't this increase their costs?

Everyone seems to be obediently going about their day-to-day lives, going to school when they're supposed to. It seems like companies are doing the same thing, but sometimes they lose money and claim they need to reduce the workforce. The state is also doing what it's supposed to do; they need so many graduates to be absorbed. At the moment I'm not exactly sure who should take responsibility, but it absolutely is not my problem. I'm not shouldering the blame.

The 996 schedule is really serious and so oppressive.* People don't have any space for their own lives. Those jobs that are a bit more relaxed will have lower salaries and a lot of BS to deal with. I have some friends who've become civil servants, and their salaries are really low. They pay their mortgage and then there's already nothing left. And there is so much nonsense. If the leader is sick you have to go and care for them, and then go to one event after another. I've looked at job ads and a lot of them are for positions that require certain degrees and skills, but the wages aren't as good as if you went to wash dishes in a restaurant.

For example, the company I used to work for was constantly changing their performance evaluations. They made it so that your wages are linked to your overtime. If I remember correctly, I had a colleague who did overtime basically every day, and they got 2,000 yuan per month. If the company has this kind of requirement, does it mean that everyone has to do overtime? I had a very clear sense at the time that the managers were staying later than others. Every time you went to leave work, others would say, "Did you finish that piece of work?" And your manager would say, "You're already leaving?" It made you feel unfree.

Some people really don't have a choice. The manager cussed out some middle-aged people; he said some really

---

* A 996 schedule means working 9 a.m. to 9 p.m., six days a week.

ugly things. But they just have to take it and do whatever they're told. They have to support elders and kids, so they need to accept being bossed around. Us young people really hate those workers who collaborate with management. When we start work, we have to do military drills and chant slogans, and we'll quietly curse whoever chants enthusiastically. Lots of people are starting to develop the will to resist. I think we need a lot of people to understand that involution is wrong, that things shouldn't be this way, and then start to resist.

My old company required us to go to work on May Day, so a lot of people called the labor inspection team to report this issue. I also called the mayor's hotline, and the person that took my call seemed pretty patient and like they wouldn't be afraid of a company. They very patiently explained to me what we should do, and I felt like it was respectful. Some of the steps required us to register using our real names, so we asked friends to file reports on our behalf. These reports were successful and when the company received the notification, they said we didn't have to come in. The info about the people who reported was not leaked. This thing was just too brazen, asking us to do overtime on May Day, a legal holiday. Of course it isn't allowed, especially for a publicly listed company. It's so bad for their reputation.

But if it's a less visible form of overtime, then it's very hard to address. If you ask them, they'll just say, "If you think there's a problem with your wages, then take your pay slip and overtime records and apply for labor arbitration, and maybe they'll arbitrate." I haven't tried to do this.

In my cohort of recruits there was an intern who was accused of switching workstations without permission. After that they were fired. They went to labor arbitration and won; the company had to pay compensation. Later, HR told us not to file these kinds of cases; that it might leave a criminal record or something.

I'm somewhat familiar with other grievance channels, like unions, but my old company didn't have a union. You can also post stuff on the internet like on Zhihu or Zhaopin.* A lot of my colleagues post their complaints about the company in various comment sections, and its scores are quite low. This led to HR purchasing a Zhihu membership, and they hired people to delete and manipulate the comments sections, but it didn't work. A lot of new employees will search for info on the company, and its reputation is already repellant. There's not much the company can do; this is a way for us to resist using just our relatively quiet and weak voices.

As far as I know, there isn't any gender discrimination in the industry. They treat everyone equally—like dogs. The top boss is a man, but the recruitment department prefers to hire women, because women are more careful. They won't be so brave in crossing various red lines. Procurement officers also need to be sensitive to finances and courageous in negotiating with others. There isn't gender discrimination, but nobody will look after you.

* Zhaopin is an employment recruitment site.

Our Company Is Quite Rigid, and I Want to Work for a Foreign Firm

I didn't feel like there was much workplace intrigue at my last job, we just focused on business and got things done. They just wanted efficiency and wouldn't even use any corporate jargon. In this industry you say whatever you have to, there's no need to lie or speak in platitudes. Everyone just wants to see results. They have a saying, "I don't want to hear a story." For example, you might have had to go through all kinds of frustrating twists and turns to finalize a contract, but your manager won't say anything about how you had to deal with all these difficulties. He'll just ask how much money you saved and when the products will arrive. This is what things were like internally at the company. You also have to learn how to hide things, how to keep an ace up your sleeve, and how to have a particular way of speaking. There's lots of info you can't divulge, so you need to learn these skills.

I felt like people were pretty cold at my old job. We did overtime together and would just talk about work issues, so people came and left quickly. I basically haven't kept in touch with any of my old colleagues since I left, and nobody has asked how I'm doing.

The company I'm at now was originally part of an SOE, and there are still a lot of connections. The vibe is a bit like an SOE. We have forty or fifty people in the company; there are only three or four who are the same age as me. The rest were born in the '70s or '80s, and among the older workers, females are in the majority. Usually they talk about whatever they've eaten that day, or which supermarkets are having a sale, or about having kids, or houses and cars. They know a lot about everyone's family life. There are these two women in my office who even know how much the other has left to pay on their mortgage, how old their kids are, what the kids like to eat. They know everything about each other, and their lives are quite interwoven.

Since I'm younger I mostly just keep quiet, I don't want to say too much. They're older than me, so if they're talking about their kids' education and I have a different opinion, I won't say anything. I also don't say anything when they talk about having kids. When they're complaining about their kids or husbands, I just laugh along. I think these women are quite friendly, though sometimes they can also be severe. But overall, they are warm and considerate, so I feel like I need to be well behaved and things will be all right.

I want to work for a foreign company but based on the info I have from suppliers I've worked with in the past, they are also pretty strict. And because the domestic market is already pretty chaotic, it's not that easy to go work for a foreign company. Labor rights protection in foreign firms is done by the book. I have a friend in K City who works for a foreign company. They start work at 10 a.m. and finish at 5:30, they get a lunch break every day, and the company provides snacks. Then they'll organize various kinds of activities for special interests—for example, to protect the environment or support LGBTQ people—or eating and drinking events. It's quite an enriching environment. My company is quite rigid; maybe foreign companies are a bit more innovative. My friend also has a lot of paid vacation days, which they can accumulate. They can take ten days off at a time, and if it's too hot they can work from home. I'm pretty envious.

But business is not great for foreign companies right now. Nobody has money now and there is pretty serious belt-tightening. People will choose to use domestic products if possible. Foreign companies have a lot of costs that can't be cut without major impact. Since the start of the war in Ukraine a lot of foreign companies have had their supply chains broken; they can't get microchips. With foreign companies unable to get supplies, the whole market has been upended, so there's more purchasing of domestic products. At the time, foreign industrial companies received a shock. I work at a distributor for a foreign company and I can tell that it's a buyer's market, so we'll have to see how things go in the future.

Now, I Believe in Quality of Life

I feel like from when I graduated till now, I've just been going with the flow. I was still quite ignorant about my own specialization when I graduated. When I was looking for work, I'd just look at recruitment posters to see what kind of specialization they were interested in, and I never really thought that I could do procurement. And I never thought that I would keep doing procurement in my second job, maybe I'm just locked into to this path.

Now, I believe in living, or in the quality of life. I need to do some emotional adjustments each day and maintain some hope, and maybe I'll survive till retirement.

After retirement I can try something else, or maybe I'll wait a while and the market will relax a bit. Or if I can get some savings, then I can leave this stuff behind and do something else. You need to have some aspirations for yourself, to keep developing yourself to do more stuff. At a minimum I want to escape the predicament of going to work every day, it is exhausting. I don't want to go to work, really.

8

A Nonessential Social Work Graduate: The First to Be Optimized

I did undergrad at a regular school and majored in auto engineering. For grad school I went to what counts as a top-tier university and finished my master's degree in social work in 2021. The auto industry touches on a lot of different areas like batteries, data, electric power, and other specialized fields of knowledge. In my undergrad studies they only taught us some general knowledge, we didn't do any detailed investigations. When I was an undergrad I did an internship at Tesla, and after graduation I went to the national job fair. I was hired by a domestic auto company and it went pretty smoothly, but the compensation wasn't good enough. I tried working there for a while but then quit, and now I'm looking for work.

Social work graduate Xiao Ma,
2021 master's degree, looking for work

It was a long time between when I started to prepare for the grad school exam and when I was finally admitted. At first, I wanted to study computer science, but the past few years the IT industry has been pretty involuted. Starting a program at that moment would have been extremely difficult so I gave it up and applied to social work programs. I only knew a little bit about social work, and its biggest attraction was that it was easy to pass the exam. I was targeting a top-tier school, so it was a way to improve my educational credentials. I did some internships while in grad school, which is when I realized that within the current system, social work is expendable. So it was a very confusing phase for me. I didn't know what my future employment and professional prospects would be like with this major.

I did a program in grad school that was focused on helping kids, and at least it gave me some sense of accomplishment. But these internship experiences did nothing to change my post-graduation situation; I couldn't use this major to find relevant work. I was a little disappointed, but I don't regret choosing this major. I really was able to change things for some people, and graduate study was a meaningful experience in and of itself. For me personally, it was a realization of my own life values.

Our teacher explained it to us very clearly: Those who do well after graduation get to be civil servants; they've reached the pinnacle of life. Those who do poorly will be street-level community workers. I was confused at the time. I stayed at home for a while and submitted some résumés and tried to get a job in an auto company based on my undergrad degree. But the domestic auto industry isn't doing well now, so that hasn't produced any results.

Looking for Work for More Than Half a Year

It's already been more than six months since I started applying for jobs. When I finished my grad degree it was right during the pandemic, so I went back home to take a breather. Later I realized that aside from me, everyone else from my major was taking the civil service exam. A lot of students in this major have an inclination toward the civil service. I wasn't that interested, so I never planned on taking the exam. When I started applying for jobs, I discovered that my major didn't fit the job requirements.

The ideal for social work graduates is to go help marginalized social groups; we want to help people who have encountered some obstacles to having a normal life. But one of the reasons I went to grad school was to escape having to find work. It wasn't that easy to find work then, and I wanted to improve myself by getting an academic credential. But after finishing this degree I realized it isn't that useful and doesn't have many prospects.

A lot of my classmates started preparing for the civil service exam as soon as they got into grad school; it's super competitive. The success rate is about fifty-fifty, and within China that's not too bad. It is a first-rate school after all. While I was in grad school I was focused on gaining life experience and doing public service programs; I wasn't very interested in the civil service exam. Those people who made up their minds to take the exam early on had to compete against people from other elite schools around the country. If they are trying to be civil servants—of course they're focused on getting to the central government, or maybe some large cities—the competition is between people from Tsinghua, Peking University, Fudan, and Jiaotong.*

My Ideal Job Is in a Foreign Company in a First-Tier City

My ideal job is in a first-tier city. I was an undergrad in a big first-tier city, and I'd like to work in this kind of city. A lot of young people, myself included, have this kind of attraction to first-tier cities. They're trying to throw off their economic circumstances to fulfill their yearning for a bourgeois life; a yearning to go out and live it up. We also like the inclusiveness of big cities toward young people.

People around my age will have to deal with family pressure to get married if they stay at home. In small cities, people are quite intolerant of your interests, behavior, and your ideals. Nobody is going to mind you in a big city; everyone is busy with their own lives, and you can find like-minded people who share your interests.

I was more interested in foreign companies than private domestic companies when I was looking for work. Foreign companies see you as a human. They are much better than domestic companies when it comes to working hours, social security, and a whole bunch of benefits, and there's also less stress. In the current environment, a lot of domestic companies are just following the lead of foreign companies—this is true for their management style and for their technology. To be honest, they're just copying others.

---

* These are among the most elite universities in China.

But these domestic companies are poor copies. They have the stress of foreign companies but without the same benefits. Instead, they'll demand that you blend Chinese and foreign culture, and require some things that make you feel uncomfortable. Domestic private companies are a classic example of "lots of work for little pay," and they don't even see you as human.

The reality is that foreign companies aren't "high pay for little work." I'm just saying that given the system, they'll give employees some space to develop, allowing them to have a bit of their own life. In foreign companies you don't have to deal with work stuff after work hours. But in some domestic companies you might still need to respond to emails and your manager's texts. Even if it doesn't affect your life, it will influence your mood. Workers might need to always be staring at their phones, and then if your manager is looking for you, you definitely have to respond to their texts. It's the same as coerced overtime, but it doesn't even count as actual overtime. It's purely working as the manager's secretary during nonwork hours, to respond to their individual needs. This is a cultural gap. Why is the manager looking for us in the evenings? It could be that the manager's manager is just pushing them. The reality is there is a whole chain, everyone is being impacted by this kind of culture. Foreign companies pay a bit more attention to work-life balance; life is life, work is work, you can make a clear distinction.

Social Work Has Become Expendable

The majority of my classmates from grad school took the civil service exam. Very few social work majors can find work in our field. While we were in school, they'd talk about how there isn't much help that social workers can provide, given the current situation in China. As I've said, we help seniors, youth, children, and some disabled people.

But to be honest, we don't have our own sources of funding; all these social resources come from the state. So of course it's the state that has to resolve these social problems. Since we can't distribute these social resources, we can't directly resolve these problems. We mostly help people coordinate with relevant government agencies like the Bureau of Civil Affairs or the All-China Women's Federation. We'll also work with foundations or public interest groups to provide some help when individuals have a specific issue. Us social workers only play a coordinating role. So under these social conditions we're just an extra link in the whole process.

Take for example an isolated elder; the way to directly address his situation is to provide basic welfare.* The Bureau of Civil Affairs and streel-level officials should be the ones doing his background check and distributing benefits. We just play a coordinating role, so under our current social system, our existence is expendable.

I don't think my failure to find work reflects a problem with my major; this is an inevitable period of national

---

* 低保.

economic slowdown. One of the subfields for us social workers is corporate social responsibility where we serve company employees. But if you pay close attention, you can tell that this is a department that the company doesn't really need. If the company needs to do some optimization, people in our field will be the first to be optimized. This is because of their lack of impact on the functioning of the company. If the people who do internal community service work leave, the company can still get by. It can still produce goods and conduct trade. The company won't have this kind of approach for positions that cannot be replaced.

Because the economy is declining, lots of companies are in bad shape. Everyone is doing layoffs to their hearts' content and cutting back on recruitment. So it's inevitable that they'll hire fewer people like us in service positions; things will naturally be hard for us. There are many structural problems that have made it harder to find a job. People I know that are the same age or are from the same generation have had similar feelings. My high school classmates have not done well on the job market; they're all in flexible employment. I've applied for work and tried some different jobs, but they're basically in sales positions. Some friends with grad degrees refuse to do sales because it's such a stressful job. Lots of people can't find a good job that suits them.

Our aim is to help socially marginalized groups. I've already mentioned how I joined some programs when I was in grad school, including programs that provide support to juvenile delinquents and elders living alone. This included material support as well as social and emotional help; the aim was to improve their lives a little bit. But these kinds of activities don't happen in foreign enterprises.

Why are so many of my classmates taking the civil service exam? They hope to have a position as a civil servant, to be paid by the state and to serve the people. But there are real limitations to this profession. There are some civil society groups now, but their organizational structure and membership is relatively traditional and extremely unenlightened, and they haven't integrated young people.

It's pretty hard to find work that aligns with your major. I have a classmate who didn't want to take the civil service exam after graduation. After she looked for work for a while, her outcome was more or less the same as mine. She couldn't find any appropriate work, and after looking for more than half a year she took a job working in HR. There is no connection at all between HR and our major. Maybe the company was just looking at her degree and thought that they could gradually train her. This means that she won't be using any of the knowledge she gained in grad school.

When I was interviewing for grad school, the professor asked me what I knew about social work. I remember that I had some lofty words about "serving marginalized communities" and things like that. The teacher who was interviewing me, who later became my advisor, responded, "You're overly idealistic, you'll understand after you graduate." I became his student and just before I wrote my thesis, he asked me what I had learned about social work. I told him, "It's hard to find a job doing social work," and he said, "You finally understand! Go ask any of your classmates, they're all prepping for the civil service exam. Seems like you're the only one relaxing." I told him he was right, and he said, "If you don't prep for the civil service exam, then you won't find a relevant job. Trying to be a civil servant is the best choice, because after this you won't have to think about work anymore."

I told him that I understood, but at the time I didn't *really* understand. It wasn't until I was looking for work that I truly understood: The reality for social work students is we cannot find relevant work outside of the state system; we have to find a different path.

The Government Should Use State Policy to Smash Involution

I think that the government bears the greatest responsibility for youth unemployment. The government hasn't used strong policies to protect labor and to smash involution.

The first major reason for unemployment is the education system. Maybe you've already noticed that nowadays there are undergraduates everywhere. Like with my engineering major, the government's policy used to be that a group of people would get undergrad degrees and another group would go to technical schools. The technical schools would distribute people and train them as workers and technicians. This plan has still not been realized; now everyone is going to university, which means that people with these degrees are absolutely everywhere. It's so hard to find a good job just on the basis of having an undergrad degree. People coming out of the education system have become replaceable labor power. The response should be to train more people to join industry rather than to create replaceable labor power. When the economy is doing well, then maybe companies will have money for social workers who will allow the department to perform a bit faster. But if the team is still functioning after you're gone, then you are expendable. To be blunt, our university has established a lot of superfluous degrees; these are backward majors that will be quickly superseded. With this kind of backward education system, the graduates who are coming out will have an even harder time finding work.

Then there is also social pressure to consume. If a young person finishes undergrad at twenty-two and grad school at twenty-five, then they'll have to think about getting married and having a family. In this society you need to have a house, a car, and savings. There is a trend among young people to ignore these things, but my parents' generation won't allow that to happen. And my family has only limited resources to support me. Like, I want to find work and settle down in a big city, but the realities of life mean that I won't be able to spend my whole life there. Lots of young people are dealing with the same kind of problem.

The third issue is that we're on a similar road as Japan. I've done some research on what happened in 1998 when Japan was having an economic crisis.* They also had lots of involution and young people were leaving the big cities and

* Japan's economic crisis began in 1990, although the effects were long-lasting.

going back to their hometowns. Japan's policy response was to do lots of infrastructure investment, but it didn't resolve the problem. A lot of young people who went back home discovered that they couldn't find work to support themselves; they couldn't stay in their hometowns. Later, Japan forced a property devaluation to allow young people to return to big cities. But one of the effects of the economic crisis was that Japanese people had lost faith in the economy, and these young people adopted a low-aspiration lifestyle. This is like our current situation.

If you want young people to find acceptable jobs, there needs to be a way for people to move between different industries rather than becoming replaceable labor power. I think that after China's bubble has popped and the country goes through a lost decade like Japan, young people here will face a similar fate. All countries have to follow a similar path, beginning with high-speed growth, like with Japan's rapid postwar economic development. But all of this prosperity is actually fake, and later there will be growth bottlenecks.

But we also are different from Japan. Japan has some high-tech production, but China doesn't have this kind of foundation. Like these days we'll joke around, saying, "Light industry is live streaming, heavy industry is barbecue." China doesn't have as much high technology as Japan to allow our economy to keep going. Our economic growth in recent years has been very reliant on real estate. If we stall out here, then we'll be stuck for a long time and this will impact everyone. The simplest outcome is that if you have less money then you spend less. This means your aspirations will be lowered, right? So I think we'll fall into a "low aspiration" social dynamic like Japan.

"Disposable Batteries"

My parents haven't pressured me to find a job. My family is reasonably well-off for China; they're not super anxious about me getting work. I'm living with my parents now, so my basic expenses are covered.

I've heard that other parents pressure their kids to find work. Sometimes their kids are super anxious and will apply to any job. Some of my friends' parents say, "Don't worry if the salary and benefits are bad, they'll go up eventually. Rome wasn't built in a day, you have to start from the bottom and work your way up." This kind of attitude is because our parents' generation doesn't understand our position. When they were young there weren't concepts like "optimization."

One time I was talking to my parents, and I explained it like this: "I'm not going to be twenty-two forever, but there will always be twenty-two-year-olds." Lots of domestic companies only need one leader, like a technician to manage a group of recent college graduates, and they'll be fine. As long as they are obedient, they can complete their tasks. Lots of companies will be fine with just one capable person to manage others who are obedient and willing to work.

If I had to be one of these underlings, and didn't become a technician or a manager, then it's only natural that I would be "optimized." I'd be replaced by a recent college grad. When these students are new on the job they don't have much work experience, their wages are low, and they're willing to work. They're also more naïve.

Another important issue is that many recent university graduates have this fantasy about life in the big city. As I mentioned, I went to university in a big first-tier city. A lot of my classmates from middle and high school who went to university in some inland cities have these kinds of fantasies. You can't say that this is pure migration; people think that moving for work is really meaningful.* One generation after another of young people has this urban fantasy, imagining themselves as a character in some work of literature or film, coming to the big city. Even if they just come for one or two years, they are fresh blood for the city; they can do low-end labor for some company.

For a company to complete its tasks, it just needs one technician to oversee the labor of this group of ambitious and naïve university graduates. There is an endless supply of "disposable batteries" to lure into the workplace.

I Want Work that Gives Me a Sense of Accomplishment

My ideal situation is to have freedom to organize my work time. I'd like to come to work a little bit late in the morning and leave a little early in the afternoon. When there's more work to be done, I could come in, but I could be around even if there isn't much happening. There's something else, though: I often think about how most people are

* The meaning is unclear in the original (纯粹移民), but it suggests migration just for economic reasons.

looking for work to earn money to live. But they're overlooking the sense of satisfaction and accomplishment you can get from work. Like I said before, when I was a grad student, taking part in various programs gave me a sense of accomplishment.

Is there a difference between someone at work thinking, "I'm just doing this to earn some money," and them thinking, "I'm willing to eat shit for money"? Right?! To be honest I want to do work that gives me a sense of accomplishment and can make me feel happy. For me, that comes from helping others, which is why I chose this major. I want to be able to help others and make their lives a little better. This is the most important thing for me, but not too many people think this way. I feel like this is just my perspective. Like I said, my family is well enough off that at least I don't have to worry about having enough to eat.

It might be that a lot of people do have to worry about having enough to eat and they aren't thinking about having a sense of accomplishment, work is just work. I hope we can all find a sense of accomplishment.

Lying Flat Is the Only Way to Avoid Involution

I just gave the example of how our predecessors in Japan fell into a morass with no way to extricate themselves. If we face the same kind of problem there will be no precedent, we'll just have to try things out. But experimenting requires time, and it will consume the time of our generation in exchange for a better life for the next generation or the one after that. But people only get one life, right?

Who would consent to having their life consumed like this? Given this situation, lying flat is the only way to avoid involution. I think that since social conditions are like this then I'll just quit, I'll do whatever makes me happy. I'm like those "Sanhe Gods" you see on the internet, working one day at a time, doing whatever I please.* After work, just going online and eating the cheapest food.

If I'm trying to stand out from the crowd and make a mark in this society, then involution is unavoidable. I'll have to get more degrees, improve my skills, improve my knowledge. Then to become an industry leader I'd have to take down lots of other people before I could finally seize the things I desire. My assessment is that there is no way to solve these social problems right now. We're only going to see an intensification of these contradictions, including with wealth inequality, the level of involution and educational development, and at various levels of life. There is no way to resolve these things.

I am personally not going to take part in this involution. If I can't find work, then I will lie flat at home. I'm not going to sacrifice my standards, even if it means not having work. I'm not going to do a job that doesn't meet my standards.

My understanding of "lying flat" is related to what I was just saying about my views on employment. If there's more

---

* This refers to a subculture that emerged in Sanhe, Shenzhen. The "Sanhe Gods" eschew the pursuit of professional and material success, preferring to work as little as possible to sustain a low-consumption, alternative lifestyle.

money, then I can try it out; if there's a sense of accomplishment, I can also try it out. But if I'm going to compromise and I find a job that doesn't pay well and there's no sense of accomplishment, then why do I have to take this job? Should I accept pathetic wages while not even realizing my own values?

Editors' Afterword

I think that the interviews and writing for this report on youth unemployment went very smoothly. Our interviewees were quite cooperative, even when we asked some sensitive questions; they did their best to respond. But there were some issues. Whenever we prepared the interview transcripts it felt like there were some questions that we should have explored further. Maybe we just didn't have enough experience.

I was unemployed while I was doing these interviews. I officially started to look for work in mid-September of last year when I began applying to some domestic companies. My master's degree is from a highly ranked university so my friends and cousins must have had high hopes for me. The result was that I applied for a lot of jobs but didn't get anything. Ultimately, I applied for four hundred jobs and got almost ten interviews. Back in the day you could get a 300k pay package, but there's no hope of that anymore.

kobayashi

Before starting this, I never would have thought that it would turn out to be such a huge project. Doing the interviews and processing the transcripts took a lot longer than expected. First, we had to produce the transcript, and then edit and condense it before reordering things. If we do similar projects in the future, I'd like to see some comparative graphs, like changes in the youth unemployment rate.

I had a lot of feelings while doing the interviews. Like a lot of the interviewees said, it's not that they can't find a job, but rather that involution is so serious: Either you accept extremely low wages, or fight tooth and nail in the civil service exam, or do 996-level overtime. It makes you feel really helpless; people don't know what to do. As for myself, I'm still a student and doing some occasional part-time work. I think I'm a little different from the interviewees. The economy is slowing in Europe now, and there are issues with unemployment and involution that I worry about. But I think this can't compare with the situation in China.

Yi Jiu (一九)

When we contacted the interviewees, I felt so lucky that they trusted me. It allowed me to hear about the individual experiences of the people behind the survey responses. The three people that I interviewed all had different experiences looking for jobs and being employed. But across the various industries they had points in common, including concerns with the instability of employment, critiques of the employment situation and conditions in their industry, examinations of the content of their work and its meaning, and descriptions of the stress that comes from an awareness of crisis. People out of work were sometimes unwilling to be interviewed and provided various explanations, which is completely understandable. People with jobs had also been through a long struggle with applications, and the pay and benefits they ended up with were quite bad.

Hearing people talk about their experiences also made me reflect on my own situation. It gave me newfound strength but also made me feel a kind of ineffable sense of helplessness. They are like me and my friends: twenty-somethings at the margins of regression and crisis. We're bearing our families' expectations to have a family and a career. Even if you're willing to exchange your body, labor power, skills, and time for the means of survival, there are no channels or space for discussion, nobody who is willing to resolve the problem. Within this process there are already some that have claimed the resources and the right to speak: Companies, schools, and government departments claim this responsibility for themselves. And they will not admit the abnormalities of the market, education, and labor systems, and how each exploits young people.

Looking back on it, after the government stopped reporting data on youth unemployment, they left the masses to figure things out based on their lived experience. As labor infrastructure didn't improve across various industries, this only increased my sense of helplessness and rage. We may inevitably encounter these problems when dealing with the issue of youth unemployment. I hope that readers will continue to follow this issue after learning about the experiences of these interviewees. We need to give ourselves and others space and support.

Yu Yuan (芋圆)

I've always thought that worker voices are not adequately represented in the media, they are usually *being* represented or paraphrased. It was reported last June that the youth unemployment rate had surpassed 20 percent, then in early August the National Bureau of Statistics said they were going to stop reporting these numbers. On top of this, the government is always condescendingly telling young people what to do, but without any sense of responsibility on their part. So I was really looking forward to this survey investigation because it allowed us to listen to people directly. Even though we could only reach a limited number of people, it is still recording a part of historical reality. The participants and interviewees were more enthusiastic than I had expected. Seeing this response let me understand more clearly the difficulty of finding employment and the cruelty of the job market. It's quite disheartening that individual effort seems not to be that important in this bad environment.

I really liked doing this survey investigation and turning it into a printed volume. Perhaps there is no way to change reality, but I hope that at least it can be accurately recorded.

Tang Xin Dan (溏心蛋)

I wrote the preface to one chapter and edited a couple interviews. My personal feelings mostly come from reading the interview transcripts. These interview materials have given me a deeper understanding of youth unemployment. There are two points that really struck me. First is the "blue collarization of white-collar work." Things that were previously thought to pertain to blue-collar work—low wages, mechanized and repetitive work, excessive overtime—have become the reality for a portion of university student interns. In the past, the expectation was that you could get a dignified job with a university degree, but today that is no longer guaranteed. And the second issue is young people's political realignment. In the interview materials you can clearly feel young people's dissatisfaction with their lives. And this dissatisfaction has produced changes in their expectations for the future. For example, they are clearly much more negative about marriage and kids. Some young people see "no marriage, no kids"* as a form of resistance. This dissatisfaction has also given rise to changes in young people's political consciousness. Some of the interviewees attribute current problems to inaction on the part of the government; they think the government needs to take primary responsibility. They've expressed dissatisfaction with the political status quo.

kk Gan Lan (*kk*橄榄)

My deepest impression after doing the interviews was that each interviewee was unique, and yet they had many points in common. Young people born into regular families have been put into an education system that has meticulously transformed them into various kinds of "human talent." And then, at the moment of graduation, they are abandoned in a labor market where they must sink or swim. It seems like there are many professions for young people to choose, but the reality is that they often have no choice. Individual interests, strengths, and ideals are consumed by the imperative of survival. In the face of intense

---

* 不婚不育.

competition and a gradually deteriorating employment landscape, aside from involution and lying flat, interviewees have also thought about how they can ultimately change these common difficulties they are confronting.

Tu Zi (兔子)

There was one person who was quite willing to be interviewed but suddenly became very cautious before publication. He asked that we not publish the interview, and ultimately we agreed to leave his section out. I thought that it would be good to include his interview; even though he criticized the unemployment situation, everything he said was true. It might have been that he had just found a job and wanted stability. It's too bad because in the interview he talked about wanting to take on a side job because his salary was too low. Other interviewees didn't talk about this too much, so we weren't able to cover this issue.

A lot of people domestically and internationally are paying attention to youth unemployment. Many believe this is about economic decline, and young people are suffering because they can't find work. But in the interviews, we see that it's not that they can't find work, or that they're unwilling to work. It's that the labor market is not providing jobs that meet the needs of young people. A lot of jobs won't even provide two days off per week or allow you to keep living in the city—if it's like this, then how can society demand that young people stop being so choosy?* So I feel like youth unemployment is a special kind of passive

* 脱下长衫.

resistance. Of course, the families of this generation of youth have some savings, and if they stay out of the labor market for a short time it won't create a subsistence crisis. This gives people the ability to wait.

I hope that this publication allows for these interviews to be preserved, and that more people will spend some time understanding the labor situation for young people. Stop shouting that they need to "take off their scholar's robe, lower their expectations, and find a job." We also shouldn't look at the youth unemployment rate and start shouting that "China is going to collapse!" Neither of these ideas are grounded in reality.

Kao Ji Tui (烤鸡腿)